DISCIPLINE

DISCIPLINE

A Sourcebook of Fifty Failsafe Techniques for Parents

JAMES WINDELL

COLLIER BOOKS

Macmillan Publishing Company   New York

Maxwell Macmillan Canada   Toronto

Maxwell Macmillan International
New York   Oxford   Singapore   Sydney

Collier Books
Macmillan Publishing Company
866 Third Avenue, New York, NY 10022

Maxwell Macmillan Canada, Inc.
1200 Eglinton Avenue East, Suite 200
Don Mills, Ontario M3C 3N1

Macmillan Publishing Company is part of the Maxwell
Communication Group of Companies.

Library of Congress Cataloging-in-Publication Data
Windell, James.
Discipline: a sourcebook of fifty failsafe techniques for parents/
James Windell.—1st Collier Books ed.
p. cm.
Includes bibliographical references.
ISBN 0-02-029931-1
1. Discipline of children—United States.   2. Behavior
modification—United States.   I. Title.
HQ770.4.W56   1991
649'.64—dc20   90-23903   CIP

Macmillan books are available at special discounts for bulk
purchases for sales promotions, premiums, fund-raising, or
educational use. For details, contact:

  Special Sales Director
  Macmillan Publishing Company
  866 Third Avenue
  New York, NY 10022

First Collier Books Edition 1991
10 9 8 7 6 5 4 3 2
Printed in the United States of America

CONTENTS

— what is Discipline
— Different forms
when we use which one
Dev. stages-ages

ACKNOWLEDGMENTS

I WOULD LIKE to extend my sincere thanks to several people who gave me emotional support throughout the writing of this book.

First and foremost is my wife, Ellen, who has always indulged my writing and allowed me to satisfy my own private muse.

Dolly Moiseeff, friend and editor, was the first person to seriously suggest I write a book about raising children. She worked with me from the inception of the ideas contained in this book and helped to give the manuscript its final shape. Her belief in me exceeded my belief in myself.

My agent, Denise Marcil, has my undying appreciation and gratitude. She believed in the book on first reading it. Her recommendations for revision were extremely helpful.

Natalie Chapman, my editor at Macmillan, has been an enthusiastic source of support from the first moment we spoke and before either of us knew that Macmillan would publish the book. She has been a joy to work with and made the crucial days of revision tolerable.

Then there are the friends who have given love and encouragement for many years. Joyce and John Ewing, Chris and Mary Bovee, Gene and Audrey Grier, Ron and Dianne Nelson, and Steve Thomas all gave of themselves, frequently and willingly listening to me talk about the book without begrudging me their time. Mary Pettit deserves special thanks for her typing, editing, and countless hours of discussion about parenthood. She has my heartfelt thanks for letting me use her successes and her concerns about her daughter, Paige, to illustrate points about discipline.

Finally, Gene Grier has to be acknowledged as the cheerleader who always rallied my spirits. His upbeat support and enthusiasm—without ever reading the manuscript—led me to do what had to be done. I cannot thank him enough.

INTRODUCTION

ANOTHER PARENTING BOOK?

Yes, but this one is different. *Discipline: A Sourcebook of Fifty Failsafe Techniques for Parents* is devoted to discipline and practical ways of dealing with children. It teaches parents how to use a wide range of discipline techniques that taken in their entirety, provide a comprehensive and understandable approach to raising children from toddlerhood to the often tumultuous teen years.

Many discipline and parent-training books take a particular point of view about discipline and suggest that all children can be dealt with by understanding and using that one view along with a limited range of discipline skills. Such books would have you believe that their approach will work for every child-discipline problem and every stage of childhood. Implicitly they suggest that the personality of your child will not make a difference in the effectiveness of their methods.

Every mother and father of more than one child knows this

just isn't so. Each child is a unique individual, and more often than not, each child in the same family, brought up by the same set of parents, reacts to life in a completely different way. The discipline or parental approach that works for one child does not work for another. The same child also changes as he* grows older. A youngster may be sullen for several years during middle childhood, only to become a bright, more easily managed child in preadolescence. Another child may seem to grow up without any problems until adolescence, and then the bottom falls out. Given the differences in children, and in the same child over the years, the child-discipline techniques you use must be adaptable to each child and each situation.

As a young father, I was nervous about raising children and wanted to be a good parent. Nothing I had learned in college or in graduate psychology classes seemed to prepare me for being a father to my own children. Like most parents, I turned to the popular parenting books.

Some were very helpful with particular problems. A couple described in elegant language their philosophy of parenting. Many talked about the importance of communication, the necessity of being firm, the ways to elicit children's cooperation.

But not one book could I find that offered the kind of complete approach to discipline and child guidance that I needed with my two unique and very different children.

My own philosophy of parenting, which I hope comes across in this book, grew out of my experiences in raising a girl (now twenty-two) and a boy (now eighteen), as well as what I've studied, read, and heard. It was also shaped by my practice as a psychotherapist working with parents and their children.

At the age of twenty-two and just out of college with an

---

*I use the personal pronouns *he* and *she* generically in alternate chapters.

undergraduate degree in psychology, I began working in a juvenile court with delinquents and their parents. I had little practical experience with the issues that concerned parents, and parents frequently asked me, "How many children do you have?" Hearing that I had none, they could then safely discard any recommendations or insight I offered them. In retrospect, I think they may have been wise to do so.

A few years later, after finishing graduate work in psychology and while working in the Oakland County, Michigan, Juvenile Court Psychological Clinic, I was assigned the task of conducting parent-training programs. That seemed easy enough; by then I had two children of my own and had also read many parenting and discipline books.

But nothing I read or knew actually prepared me to work successfully with groups of parents of delinquents. The parent-training programs that were popular, most of which emphasized increasing communication between parents and children, seemed inadequate and insipid for juvenile court parents.

I conducted a national survey of juvenile court programs to see if anyone was doing anything better that I could learn from. That didn't help. I began writing a newspaper column on parenting and discipline, which made it possible for me to hear from and talk to a great number of parents with concerns about raising children. In the meantime, I continued a clinical psychotherapy practice that dealt primarily with children and adolescents with behavior problems and their parents.

Out of this practice and the parent-training and discipline classes I continued to conduct for parents—many of whom had mistreated their children or had delinquent children they were trying to cope with—I gradually developed the ideas and methods in this book. Because I couldn't find the kind of book that I could comfortably recommend to my clients and my classes, I decided to write one. This book reflects my experiences with thousands of families, both normal and disturbed. It also owes a deep debt of gratitude to the late Dr. Fritz Redl, with whom I studied in graduate school.

Dr. Redl's expertise with delinquents and his experiences with doing on-the-spot therapy with youngsters came from his innovative Pioneer House, a residential placement for some of Detroit's worst delinquents in the late 1940s.

He often described these children and the lessons he learned dealing with them on a day-to-day basis. His classification of "influence techniques," which presented the most effective ways to apply discipline to children, has been a major influence in my own thinking about what parents need to learn to be successful.

What Dr. Redl so thoughtfully taught was that adults working with children need a bag of tricks to handle the various problems in discipline and management. I've modified and adapted his techniques for parents of children who present both usual and unusual discipline problems.

Because parents have different styles and personalities, just as their children do, it is unrealistic to think that knowing one or two discipline skills is going to get you through eighteen years of a child's life at home. A parent must have that bag of tricks ready at all times, for it will come in handy when a child gets tired of the approach you normally use, or when that technique is no longer effective, or when you forget and, somewhat like an addict, slip off the wagon of calm, rational guidance.

The parenting skills taught in this book take into consideration variations in parents' experience and attitudes. They assume that all parents will make some mistakes. By learning many parenting skills, I believe, your chances of slipping seriously are considerably reduced.

The overall philosophy of this book is that there is no single technique to use with your children. Knowing more about all of the available discipline skills will make you a better parent. However, this is not necessarily an easy approach to child rearing. You can't learn how to be an effective disciplinarian in three simple lessons; you will have to practice the skills described in the following chapters.

The good news, however, is that you *can* learn to use every skill described in this book. I know from practical experience as a father and from my work with thousands of parents that when some care is taken to learn and apply the discipline skills described here, they will work, and you will be pleased with the results.

I recommend you read the chapters in the order they appear because the earlier chapters lay the groundwork for what comes later, providing important information you need to consider before you start to discipline. Once you've read the book all the way through, keep it handy to refer back to when you encounter a new challenge with your children.

I strongly suggest you practice the techniques you learn as you go along. I often ask parents I work with to use a notebook to write down comments about various discipline skills and to keep a record of how they have used a particular technique and the results they saw. By doing this, parents can see that they have really learned the technique. They can more easily spot flaws in their ways of handling these skills, and they can better determine if a discipline skill will be effective with their children.

One final suggestion. All of us as parents fall into bad habits. We may find that we're criticizing too much, forgetting to say nice things, or threatening too often. Keeping this book handy to review every so often can be a way of reminding yourself what has worked in the past and the skills you have forgotten to use lately.

By referring to this book when you need a refresher, I hope you find this is the last discipline book you'll ever need.

ONE

How to Be a Successful Parent

"MY SEVEN-YEAR-OLD daughter has a mind of her own," said an exasperated mother. "I get so frustrated with her, I yell and I feel like spanking her. I know that's not the thing to do."

Another parent says: "My son is not a bad boy, but I have problems getting him to do what I want. I try to be calm but can't be. He pushes me to my limits."

"My daughter won't listen to me," another parent complains. "She says I'm mean or that she hates me. I tell her I love her, but that doesn't seem to make things easier. I've tried everything. What am I supposed to do?"

Sound familiar? If it does, then this book is for you. It was written with frustrated, I've-come-to-the-end-of-my-rope and I've-tried-everything-I-know parents in mind. But, unlike other parenting books, this book doesn't tell you what you *must* do in order to have compliant, well-behaved kids. Instead, I will tell you what you *could* do. That's an important difference.

You know your own child better than anyone else does. No

one else, therefore, can tell you what you should do if your child is misbehaving or presenting a new discipline problem. If you are like nearly every other parent in the United States, you have never received formal training in how to be a parent and how to use discipline effectively, so you don't know all the available discipline and child-management skills and techniques. This book describes fifty discipline skills. These skills are presented so as to provide you with enough examples and enough knowledge to use them with your children. But it will be up to you to decide when and how you use these discipline skills with your unique child.

Whether your child is stubborn, defiant, or hyperactive, whether your child acts up for attention or gets into serious trouble, this book can help you meet your parenting challenge.

Every mother or father I've ever met wished to be a perfect parent. Most of us know, however, that we fall far short. Yet we generally have in our minds a picture of what we consider the ideal or outstanding parent. Many of us even know men and women we would label as "great parents." When I ask parents to describe their image of a perfect parent, the ideal has some or all of the following characteristics:

- Always calm and in control.
- Always kind and loving to her children.
- Always able to handle discipline problems.
- Never too busy for her children.
- Always positive and optimistic with her children.
- Always knows how to respond to her children.

What separates them from their ideal, parents tend to think, is that the perfect parent can "always" handle things and is "never" unable to cope. It is true that some mothers and fathers seem to have the right instincts for understanding their children and responding appropriately when a problem occurs.

No parent, however, is really like that all the time. Most parents want to be under control more often and able to come up with a response or a discipline skill on the spot when needed.

That's what this book will teach you. After reading this book and practicing the skills described, you shouldn't ever be at a loss to know how to handle that new challenge or that new problem with your youngster.

Most times, it seems to me, parents who don't know what to do or what to say to their child are simply overwhelmed by a new problem or situation—one they've never had to face before. Or (and this seems to happen even more often) they are emotionally crippled by the implications of the behavior they see in their child.

Every parent has had this sort of thing happen at one time or another. You're in the supermarket checkout line and your son swipes a piece of gum. Or worse, as you get in the car after leaving the store, you hear the crackle of paper and see your daughter opening a candy bar that she didn't buy. What do you think? If you're a normal first-time parent, your thoughts immediately project into the future and you try to imagine how you're going to face the neighbors (not to mention your in-laws) when your daughter's name is in the newspaper for armed robbery. You're sure she's a bad seed, destined to grow up to be a disgrace to you and her family.

When my own daughter was caught smoking a cigarette in the backyard at age twelve, I was sure the next step would be car theft followed by heroin addiction. There goes my career as a psychologist, I thought. With these concerns, it was obviously impossible to respond appropriately to the relatively minor incident at hand. Impossible—when you're projecting into the future and concocting all sorts of dangerous and illegal behavior—to respond the right way.

It may be easy to say the right thing to a child who was

caught smoking, but when you have to come up with a way to handle car theft and heroin addiction, the problem is overwhelming. We often don't know the best way to act because we see ourselves as a failure as a parent and, as a consequence, our child as having serious behavior problems.

If you carefully read and understand how discipline skills are classified, you can determine the technique you need to use. By better understanding the various kinds of discipline skills and what they are likely to accomplish, you have a much better chance of picking one that will work with your child.

Being a competent parent doesn't mean you can't ever lose control or that you can't ever be mystified or stumped by a discipline problem. Nor does it mean that you can't sometimes use the wrong technique. It doesn't mean that you can't be angry or show strong emotions. Successful parents are quite human and fallible; they express real emotions; they also love and (usually) enjoy their children; and they realize that parenting is not an inborn skill.

Good parents know that they can never know enough about parenting. They know that there is always more to learn about being good mothers or fathers, and that having a bag full of skills to use with children is not only important but essential. Good parents know that in addition to patience, tolerance, understanding, and flexibility, practical skills are vital to the job of raising children.

Understanding both children and a parent's role requires the further realization that you will often face new and unexpected challenges from your kids. Just when you think you've got the job of mother or father under control, a new problem comes along that demands discipline skills that you haven't used before.

As a parent you must know how to cope with new discipline challenges. You hope that you'll never have to deal with a child who skips school, steals from a local store, is depressed over a family crisis, tries drugs, or threatens to run away. However, every parent realizes that with the challenges, temptations, and expectations kids face in our society, you can't say you'll never have to deal with these issues. When these kinds of problems occur, you have to be prepared as a parent. And you have to know enough about the science of discipline to answer the challenge.

BY DISCIPLINE, I am not just talking about punishment. I use discipline in the broad sense of the term—not the narrow sense usually restricted to ways of punishing misbehavior.

The word *discipline* comes from the word *disciple*, which means student or follower. As parents we are teachers of our children: we teach them to be self-disciplined, to be able to live well in our society, and to like themselves. It is easy to be a teacher or trainer of the young when things are going well. But it usually takes all of the skills and training we have to deal with our children when they have behavior and attitude problems.

There are a great many parenting and child discipline books available in bookstores and libraries. Most follow one of three basic approaches. One approach is the Alfred Adler–Rudolf Dreikurs approach, which teaches encouragement, democratic parenting, and a combination of natural and logical consequences to solving child-rearing problems.

Second, there is the Haim Ginott–Thomas Gordon approach, based on the best-selling books by Ginott *(Between Parent and Child)* and Gordon *(Parent Effectiveness Training)*. This approach promotes communication and disdains punishment in the belief that responding to children's underlying feelings is the right way to proceed with discipline.

The third approach is behavior modification or reward and punishment. All discipline in such books is viewed in terms of

rewarding good behavior and punishing or extinguishing unwanted behavior.

For many mothers and fathers, these three basic approaches to parenting have been helpful. For a great many
more parents, however, these approaches are too simplistic and
assume all children will respond to these techniques. The real-
ity is that rewards don't work for all children or all parents.
Similarly, a democratic style isn't compatible with many parents' personalities.

An additional problem with these traditional late-twen-
tieth-century approaches to parenting is that a large number of
parents don't become concerned about their parenting abilities
until they recognize their child has a serious problem. At that
point, it is much too late to think of applying rewards ("You
didn't smoke dope today. Good, I'll take you for some ice
cream.") or natural consequences ("You can go to school or
not. You decide if you want to graduate or stay in school
another year.").

While I certainly support the use of democratic parenting
styles, choices, and rewards (you will find these described in
this book as important discipline techniques), children often
present many types of challenges, calling for a variety of parenting skills. Using only one approach to all problems (offering
choices or giving rewards, for instance), is like cooking with
only one recipe or teaching with only one lesson plan. To deal
adequately with the variety of problems that present themselves to most parents, and to cope with the diverse personalities that make each child (and each parent) unique, parents
need a variety of skills and approaches to draw on.

The following chapters list a number of discipline and
parenting skills on which to draw when the need arises. You
need to know your child and how she reacts and what she
generally likes or dislikes. With this information, you decide

when a concern falls into one of the following categories and choose an appropriate skill from that category.

- Discipline techniques that prevent problems
- Discipline techniques that encourage self-control
- Discipline techniques that teach lessons
- Discipline techniques that encourage and reinforce appropriate and desired behaviors
- Discipline techniques that correct behavior
- Discipline techniques that discourage inappropriate and undesired behaviors

You decide what you wish to accomplish and try one of the discipline techniques described in each category. You should never be at a loss for something to do. You should never be one of those parents who say, "I've tried everything and nothing works!"

For every child-discipline problem there are dozens of potential responses. Whether your child has crossed a busy street without permission, been mean to the cat, stolen money from a neighbor, gotten into a fight on the school playground, or lied to you, there are many ways of dealing with the situation.

The philosophy of this book is based on the assumption that no one can tell you what will work best with your child. What often works well with one child in one situation will be the wrong technique to use with another child in a different situation or family.

To be the parent you want to be, you must train yourself in a variety of discipline skills. Practice these until you can use them well, and apply the skills you believe will be the most successful with your youngster. If any discipline skill you use doesn't work the way you think it should, you don't have to despair or panic. Because you will know a large number of discipline skills, you can use another or another—until one does work.

In the following chapters are all the discipline skills you'll ever need to know. It's up to you to apply them to your unique child in order to be a successful parent.

T W O

The Ten Worst
Discipline Techniques

PARENTS MAKE MANY mistakes trying to handle discipline problems. We've all used most or all of the techniques in this chapter. However common, they do nothing positive for children, with the possible exception of demonstrating we are fallible.

It's not easy to select the ten worst things we do to kids, or to limit the list to ten. Even if you can recall some of the mistakes you've made with your own children—yelling at them, embarrassing them, ordering them around, or taking your anger out on them—there are usually other parents who do far worse things. What's more, many mothers and fathers make the same mistakes over and over again. Often, it seems, they cannot break the bad parenting habits they've developed.

With my own mistakes and those of parents I've worked with in mind, I'll list the discipline techniques that qualify for a Hall of Shame for parents.

1. Physical Abuse

I'm not talking about spanking. That will be discussed in a later chapter as physical discipline. While I do not encourage spanking or swatting, I am realistic enough to know many parents consider it a legitimate discipline technique. Instead, what I am listing as number one on my Worst Discipline List is beating, hitting, slapping, punching, and otherwise physically attacking children. Today we are all more aware than ever before of how serious this is for a child's mental health and how it can lead to lowered self-esteem, behavior problems, and disturbances in adult life. Very possibly, physical abuse is strongly related to such problems in adulthood as battering of women, delinquency, crime, and assault. There is no evidence that using physical force with children does anything positive for them.

An example of a parent using excessive force that can be considered physical abuse is illustrated in a situation that happened with Mrs. Borders and her seven-year-old daughter, Melissa.

On a workday when Mrs. Borders had a new baby-sitter coming to her house to pick up her two children (she also has a six-year-old son), Melissa seemed determined to make all planning go awry. Mrs. Borders felt herself under increasing pressure as she tried to prepare for work while packing what her children needed to spend the day at the baby-sitter's house. Melissa stubbornly took a long time to change into her play clothes and then demanded to be fed.

Mrs. Borders was patient as long as she could be as she explained that they would eat at the new baby-sitter's house and that she just didn't have time to prepare anything for Melissa now. Melissa responded by crying, stamping her feet, and calling her mom a "bad mother."

"I don't care," replied Mrs. Borders. "You still have to be

ready for the baby-sitter and I'm sorry I don't have time to feed you."

When the baby-sitter pulled into the driveway a few minutes later, Melissa's brother left the house to greet her. Melissa, however, refused to go outside, continuing to verbally harass her mother. Mrs. Borders was beginning to feel desperate as she watched the clock while putting on her lipstick.

"I'm warning you," she shouted at Melissa, "go out and meet Mrs. Davis or you're going to be in big trouble!"

Melissa grabbed her backpack and screamed as she flung open the door, "I'm running away!"

That's all Mrs. Borders needed at this point. She, too, ran out of the house as Melissa headed across the front lawn. "If you leave this yard, you're going to get it!" she threatened.

Melissa kept going. "I'm going to whip you if you don't come back!" Mrs. Borders said as her son and Mrs. Davis stared at them both. Mrs. Borders was now trotting to catch up with Melissa. As she grabbed Melissa's collar, Melissa started whimpering and changed her tune.

"Okay! I'm coming back! Don't spank me!"

"Too late," she said, and with the new baby-sitter and a neighbor or two watching she hit Melissa on the behind with her purse. Melissa began wailing and ran toward the house, breaking away from her mother's grip on her coat.

Again it was a chase, with Mrs. Borders panting after her daughter and telling Melissa that she had made her late for work. She caught up to Melissa before she got to the front door. Melissa screamed, "Leave me alone, you stupid, ugly mother!"

Mrs. Borders lost it at this point. Screaming back, she began striking Melissa across the shoulders and hit her twice in the face. When Melissa fell down, Mrs. Borders jerked her up. Yelling "I'm sorry," Melissa pleaded for her mother to leave her alone as she was pulled to Mrs. Davis's car.

This is a common situation in many families when there is stress and children do not comply readily. Such spanking or beating rarely brings about anything worthwhile. Instead it causes resentment, hostility, anger, and frequently a desire to get revenge on the parent who inflicted the punishment.

2. Coercion

Closely related to physical abuse is the use of coercion. When a child does not comply with attempts to "make" him do something, parents often feel they have no alternative discipline techniques other than physical punishment or abuse.

Here's how one father used this method of bringing about compliance. Mr. Conners was at the pediatrician's office for Nathan's twice-monthly allergy injection. As they were waiting, Nathan began playing checkers with another child in the waiting room. When the nurse called Nathan's name, he pretended not to hear and continued his game.

"Go right now, young man!" Mr. Conners demanded.

"No!" said Nathan, still sitting on the floor making a new move on the board.

"I said go into the office," his father insisted, a new sense of urgency creeping into his voice. "It's your turn and you have to go."

Nathan didn't budge. He knew his father might try to pick him up, so he grabbed onto the leg of a chair. Mr. Conners got hold of Nathan's shirt and began pulling him. "Let's go," he said as he tried to pry Nathan away from the leg of the chair.

The struggle continued with Mr. Conners now threatening Nathan: "If you don't go in this minute, you're going to be in big trouble when we get home, young man!"

Nathan, recognizing he was beaten, gave in. "I hate you!" he said as he stomped off into the doctor's office.

A second way coercion is related to physical abuse is in the way kids respond to this approach. Children become angry with their parents and attempt to avoid them, their threats, and, quite often, the consequences of their own actions. Parents who use force frequently complain their children are liars or are sneaky—both natural responses to being coerced to do things we don't want to do.

3. Yelling

This is so common that I believe most parents just assume it is a useful way to get children to respond. Somehow, parents seem to think (although I wonder how much thinking goes into it) that if they increase their decibel level they have a better chance of getting compliance from their child. All of us have yelled at one time or another, and we all know that for the most part it is totally ineffective. Yet we continue to do it. Why? Probably because it's a habit or we learned it from our own parents or we need to vent anger and frustration or because it's easy. Yelling requires less time and cognitive ability than figuring out a better discipline technique to use.

Danny went to camp for a week, and while he was away his parents redecorated his bedroom. They gave the room a fresh coat of paint and on one wall put up some baseball-theme wallpaper they were sure he would like.

Danny did seem to like the new look of his room. However, a week after he got home, while doing a routine cleaning of his room, his mother discovered a hole he had made in the wall and covered over with a poster. She told her husband when he came home that evening and he let Danny have it.

"How could you do this to us! We worked really hard to fix your room for you and you treat us like dirt! I just think you are an ingrate and selfish! You don't care how hard we work or how much money we spend on you as long as you can do what you want! You're just selfish and inconsiderate!"

The verbal barrage went on for a full five minutes before he ran out of steam. Danny reacted by yelling "Shut up!" and going to his room, banging the door behind him.

It's often out of frustration or impatience that we yell at our kids. You only have to think of harried parents in stores to agree that yelling is quick and somehow makes it look as if we are doing something to deal with an unruly youngster.

The only way yelling can work is if our kids so hate to hear us raise our voices that they will respond if only we will shut up. But more often, when we yell at kids they get anxious, realize we don't know what else to do, or learn to ignore us.

4. Demanding Immediate Compliance

This technique is very closely associated with yelling. Usually the two go hand in hand. It is common to hear parents say, "I said do it now!" or "Come here this instant!" or, in the case of Mrs. North, "Chris, stop that right now!"

Chris, Mrs. North's very active six-year-old, was used to hearing his mother demand immediate compliance. "If you don't stop pushing your brother, I'm going to smack you!" she'd say. "Stop pushing him right now!"

That didn't faze Chris. So a few minutes later, Mrs. North would say, "You heard me, cut it out! Now!" Every time he did something to displease her, it was a new demand for Chris to stop his behavior "right now!" Chris, of course, rarely responded to any of these demands. This would make Mrs. North more impatient and more frantic. More demands would be followed by tugging at his sleeve and jerking on his collar. If she jerked him too hard, he would fall down and then there would be a new demand: "Stop crying this instant! I didn't hurt you! Stop it, I said!"

No self-respecting child over the age of fifteen months is going to comply instantly unless he is so intimidated and compliant that he is easy prey for a demanding parent. It seems a fact of human nature that people lose their feelings of self-respect when they comply with others who order them around or make demands for immediate action. Adults greatly resent being ordered around, and there's no reason to believe that children react differently.

5. Nagging

Of all the wrongheaded things that parents do, nagging is one of the most ineffective. This "discipline technique" also usually leads to yelling and to force. There's a good reason, too, that almost every parenting book you'll ever read will recommend firmness and consistency. When parents are firm, they rarely have to resort to nagging. Yet many mothers and fathers nag consistently.

Shawn's parents were consistent naggers. One Saturday, Shawn's mother asked him to clean his room. By Saturday afternoon, Shawn hadn't begun to touch it yet. His mother was now on his case.

"Shawn, is your room clean yet?" she asked.

"No, Mom," Shawn replied. "I'll get to it in a minute."

It wasn't fifteen minutes later before she was yelling out the same question from the kitchen. "Have you started your room yet? It's really messy and I can't stand it any longer. You'll have to do something about it today!"

"Okay," Shawn said, although he was now deeply engrossed in a video game in the family room.

"Shawn," his mother said a few minutes later, "how many times do I have to ask you to clean your room? Go start it now."

"I can't now, Ma," he groaned. "I'm right in the middle of this game. I'll get to it when this is over."

A few minutes later, his mother was beginning to sound

more annoyed and irritated. "I won't tell you again, young man. Get at your room."

An hour later, the same dialogue was still going on between Shawn and his mother. And he was no closer to starting his room than he had been that morning. Shawn got through Saturday without cleaning his room; Sunday morning his mother picked up the nagging theme once again.

Why do parents nag? Frequently because they don't know how else to get kids to do what they want, or they are timid or weak in their use of more effective discipline skills. When mothers and fathers find themselves saying, "How many times do I have to tell you to hang up your jacket?" or "Now go to bed, I'm not going to tell you again," they are nagging. But they are also failing to use other techniques that work very well. Alternatives to nagging will be given throughout this book.

6. Lecturing and Advice Giving

"You mean I can't give my favorite lecture about the value of a good education anymore?" Sorry, but that and other favorite speeches about the importance of being responsible, staying out of trouble, not smoking, and staying away from troublemakers will have to go, along with your best sermons and lectures. Why? Because kids don't listen to them.

Therefore, any advice or speech you would like to give your children that begins with any of the following is probably wasted effort:

- "What you should do is . . ."
- "If you ask me, you should . . ."
- "You have to . . ."
- "When I was your age . . ."
- "Your problem is . . ."

I think parents resort to lectures and sermons because they are so frustrated they really do not know what else to do. Mr. and Mrs. Robinson illustrate this point. They have a sixteen-year-old son who defies all their efforts to improve his grades and his attitude about school. They've tried everything they know—rewards, promises, punishment, threats. The only thing left to do, they believe, is to give him lectures and advice.

This comes easy for Mrs. Robinson, a nurse supervisor in a hospital. On her job, she commands respect from nurses and doctors. She is college educated, experienced, and well aware of the value of an education. If she could get this across to her son, she thinks, then he would progress in the way his parents want. Often both she and her husband begin long monologues to their son by saying, "You're never going to amount to anything if you don't change your attitude about school and get down to business. Who do you think will hire you if you're not well educated?"

The lectures the Robinsons give their son are always one-sided because their questions aren't really meant to be answered. And if they do want an answer, the boy's reply is usually "I dunno" or "I'll try to do better next semester." That usually stumps his parents and the only recourse they have is to proceed with the lecture.

The Robinsons have expectations and plans for their only child. It is important for them that he do well at school and go on to college. But when he doesn't live up to their expectations, they panic and think they have to take some sort of immediate action. One thing they can do immediately is give him some good advice or tell him how much better off he'd be if he listened to them.

Most children and teenagers turn off and tune out when a lecture is given. Consequently, lectures are usually a waste of time and energy. As a rule, people don't want to be told what to do. We prefer to have others listen to us and try to understand what we are experiencing. Generally, if we want advice, we'll ask for it. I feel that way. My kids feel that way. And every kid I've ever worked with in therapy feels that way—even when they are aware they are making a mistake. Kids want to make their own mistakes, not ours.

7. Taking Anger Out on Kids

This is related to lectures and yelling. As I said, parents are often frustrated because their children have let them down and are not living up to their expectations. When children have caused us great disappointment, or when difficulties, pressures, or stresses in other parts of our lives bear down on us, we sometimes jump on our kids when they do something we don't like. Then they get an extra dose of anger, criticism, punishment, or advice. Whatever it is we do or say to them at this point is usually out of proportion to their offense.

Mrs. Glick overreacted to her seven-year-old daughter, Lisa. It happened after Mrs. Glick had a problem at work and a fight with her boyfriend. She and her boss had argued over his request for her to work two hours of overtime when she was already tired. The next day, when Mrs. Glick was tired from work, angry with her boss, and confused about her relationship with her boyfriend, Lisa brought home a note from her teacher. The note described Lisa's disruptions in class and her disrespect for the teacher.

"That was the straw that broke the camel's back," Mrs. Glick explained later. "I really let Lisa have it."

What she said to her daughter went something like this:

"Lisa, how could you do this to me! This is awful. I'm embarrassed and humiliated that your teacher has to write notes to me about your behavior. Your behavior and your attitude have to change and I'm going to see to it that they do. You're grounded for three weeks. Let's see if that helps you to straighten up—although I doubt if it will the way you've been acting lately!"

Mrs. Glick knew that she had overreacted and was really taking out on her young daughter her own frustrations and accumulated anger and hurt. But it was too late.

Some of the things we say when we take out our anger and other emotions on our children injure them and damage the way they perceive themselves. I've known parents who in times of stress have said such things as "I'm sick and tired of you and the way you treat your sister!" "How could you do something so stupid?" "Sometimes I wish you were dead!" These angry statements can linger in a child's mind well into adulthood.

8. Shaming and Belittling

If we want our children to grow up emotionally strong and to like themselves, then shaming, belittling, and putting them down have no place in our repertoire of discipline techniques. I know some parents think otherwise. I will share some examples in later chapters when I list using embarrassment as a possibly legitimate technique. Here, however, I am specifically restricting my comments to those that make children feel smaller ("Why are you acting like a baby today?"), more inadequate ("I'm not going to take you shopping ever again if you can't act your age"), less intelligent ("That's one of the dumbest things you've ever done!"), and more insecure ("I can't stand you kids; I'm leaving and I don't know if I'll ever come back!"). These may sound like extreme examples; however, I hear them every day—not only from parents, but also from schoolteachers. No parent (or teacher) who truly wants children to have a solid sense of self-esteem will ever joke at a child's expense, engage in excessive teasing, or use sarcasm, put-downs, or other cutting remarks that tear down a child's feeling about himself. This also goes for setting up situations in which a child will feel embarrassed or shamed.

9. Setting Traps

This is a popular technique with autocratic and high-expectation parents. They know a child has failed to live up to a certain requirement or rule. Secure with this knowledge, they then ask the child if he has followed the rule or requirement. They are waiting for a lie or evidence that the youngster is trying to wriggle out of the situation. When this happens (because they are dealing with human beings), they pounce on the child and give him what-for because of the lie or the attempt to avoid the inevitable. Some parents become experts at this.

Mr. Buchanan is an example of a parent adept at setting traps for his children. He routinely looked through his daughter's bedroom when she was out with friends. One day he found a note that referred to marijuana use. Later that evening he engaged her in conversation. His tone sounded casual and friendly at first. Soon the direction of the discussion veered toward Bonnie's friends and their use of drugs. He than asked her if she or her friends had ever used drugs or even "talked about drugs."

When she replied, "No, we're not into that stuff," Mr. Buchanan had her trapped. He reached into his shirt pocket, tossed the note on the floor in front of her, and said, "Well, then, how do you explain this?"

There was no way for Bonnie to get out of this trap. She could lie, try to put her father on the defensive (by accusing him of being a snoop, for instance), or rail at his methods. She knew from experience that a lecture and punishment would follow, but she was determined not to let him feel that he had "beaten" her with his trap.

Bonnie is more likely—like other children whose parents set traps—to become a rebellious liar and learn to mistrust any question her father asks or any conversation he starts. The net result is a serious communication and relationship problem.

10. Imposing Excessive Guilt

Some parents are masters at making their children feel guilty. Now, I don't believe that guilt is bad. In fact, it is necessary for most of us in order to be decent and law-abiding citizens. What I'm against is excessive, crippling guilt—the kind of guilt that makes one anxious, dependent, and unable to feel free and independent.

When parents say such things as, "If you loved me, you'd obey me" or "I've devoted my life to you and what do I get in return?," they are potentially causing the kind of guilt in their children that can be very unhealthy.

Often, parents impose this guilt by making kids feel responsible for the parents' well-being. This is frequently true in dysfunctional families with an alcohol- or drug-abusing parent. Children in these families are often made to feel responsible for the parents' abuse or for taking care of them when they are incapacitated. In other families, young people are forced to feel responsible for marital problems, a parent's mental health ("You kids are driving me crazy!"), or a parent's hard work or stress.

This happened frequently in the Wilson family. Mr. Wilson had a nine-year-old daughter from his first marriage when he and the second Mrs. Wilson got married. Although his daughter, Becky, visited only on weekends, it was enough time to impose guilt feelings on her.

The new Mrs. Wilson usually instigated the guilt. The following incident was just one time when Becky ended up feeling as if she had done something to ruin things in the family. It was a Sunday afternoon and Becky was throwing a hard rubber ball for the cat to chase. Sometimes Becky's aim wasn't very good. She knocked over a vase (fortunately without breaking it) and came dangerously close to a lamp. Becky's stepmother asked her to be more careful, but Becky's father was reading the paper and offered no support.

When the ball was finally thrown in the wrong direction and hit a glass on the coffee table, Mrs. Wilson had had it. She stormed out of the house and got into her car. She gunned the engine and drove away leaving father and daughter looking at each other.

"Where did Helen go?" Becky asked her father.

"I guess she was mad at you," he said. "I don't know why you have to do things to aggravate her. I try to make Sundays pleasant for all of us and you have to spoil them."

For Becky to have to bear guilt for the emotions of her father and stepmother is both unfair and unhealthy. Over the long run, this imposition of guilt is likely to lead Becky to be overly sensitive and dependent on their moods.

THESE ARE TEN of the worst approaches to discipline. All are ineffective and frequently lead to emotional and behavioral problems in young people. Yet all parents have used at least one of these ways of handling children.

These "bad" parenting habits can be changed. The rest of this book is devoted to presenting alternative discipline techniques so that you need never have to use any of these ten worst discipline methods again.

THREE

Before You Start to Discipline

DISCIPLINE IS NOT something you start on a particular day or begin when you discover a problem with your child. You don't suddenly wake up and say, "By golly, I've got a willful five-year-old and now I've got to set some rules before things get worse." If that's the way you operate, you're in big trouble as a parent.

Why? Because you haven't set the tone or established an atmosphere for discipline. In working with parents, I've encountered many who could tolerate a lot of misbehavior until their child became a teenager. When they saw how mobile their teen was becoming, it frightened them so much they set new rules. But because they had not done so previously, they had a major rebellion on their hands.

Eighteen-year-old Susan was an example of this. She was fairly responsible for most of her teen years, but recently her parents discovered that when she said she was staying over night with a girlfriend, she was really spending time with a new boyfriend.

Her parents reacted with shock and indignation. They thought punishment was in order. But they had not had occasion to use many punishments over the years, and when they took her car away, Susan was angry and left home to stay with a friend for several days.

Susan's parents wanted to impress on her that their rule was that she had to be where she said she was going to be. But Susan's contention was, "Why make this rule for me now?" She said that she wouldn't allow such rules; after all, she was eighteen years old.

The fact is, parents begin to discipline and guide their children at birth—no matter how weakly or insecurely. For most of us, concern and an atmosphere of parental guidance starts with loving, nurturing behavior as soon as the child is home from the hospital. That behavior includes touching, holding, breast-feeding, cuddling, and cooing.

In order to set the stage for effective discipline and guidance, these things must occur during infancy. Children must feel secure and develop a sense of trust. They must have a positive outlook on the world and on the motives of others.

Will they regard the world with suspicion? Will they mistrust the motives of others? Choose to withdraw? Regard others with hostility? React to the problems they face with depression or by giving up? How your child comes to view the world and the people in it depends largely on you. In the beginning, the world—to your child—is you.

If you are there to meet their needs, hold them when they cry, feed them when they're hungry, comfort them when they're frightened, calm them when they awake at night, and play with them when they're energetic, children have the opportunity to see the world as a friendly, secure place to be.

All of this sets the tone for later guidance and discipline. A child must love her parents in order for guidance and discipline to be effective. This is especially true during the preteen and adolescent years. Children must sense that you love them and have their best interest at heart. If they don't feel this, they will not respond to your directions and teachings.

When does discipline actually start? It starts with the way you deal with your baby's needs and discomforts. It starts when you take her age and developmental level into account when she doesn't sleep the night through during the first six months. It starts when you tolerate a one-year-old spitting baby food or spilling milk. It starts when you accept the way children are and understand that children of all ages have their own sets of fears and specific developmental tasks to accomplish; that toddlers like to say "No!" and preschoolers sometimes say "I hate you!"

A large part of being a competent parent involves having goals and directions for your child. That's part of discipline and guidance, too. Competent parents have an idea of what they want for their child. But what they want and the goals they set are realistic and well within the physical and emotional abilities of their child.

Most parents these days realize how vital it is for our children to be happy, productive, and well adjusted. We also recognize that to have a child who is productive and happy, that child must have a positive sense of self-worth. Children must like themselves in order to have self-confidence and motivation.

How do parents bring this about? Parents can contribute to children's self-esteem by being good, competent disciplinarians, by giving guidance and being positive at the same time. If this sounds like a tall order, it is. But it can be done. It requires that discipline be related to love and nurturing, and that parents have a healthy respect for children and their needs at all developmental levels.

You are in a good position to be this kind of mother or father if you have good self-esteem yourself. How do you know if you have a positive sense of self-worth as a person and a parent? For one thing, you know how you feel when you try new things or go into strange situations. You know whether you feel self-confidence in talking to people, or whether you have too many fears and anxieties. Most important, you know whether you like yourself, the way you look, and the way you act with others; you know whether you enjoy life.

If you can feel good about yourself, you have good self-esteem. Parents who have high self-esteem have definite values and beliefs. They know what they believe in and are not afraid to let others know. They have a strong belief in what is right in the way they behave, dress, and treat others.

This book was written to help mothers and fathers increase their own self-esteem and the self-esteem of their children. If you as a parent have a low level of self-worth, neither this book nor any other self-help book is going to transform you into a positive, self-confident parent. Certainly what you learn from this book can help you as a parent. But you may need to see a counselor or psychotherapist for more help to increase your basic feelings of self-esteem before you can work on aspects of parenting. I happen to think your child is worth this kind of investment in time, energy, and money!

One of the ways that following the suggestions in this book will make you a more confident and able parent is by giving you various methods of presenting and enforcing your beliefs and values. You may already know what kind of behavior you want from your child, but you may not always know how best to bring this about. If you are not sure about the behavior and skills you would like from your child, you might start by reading some of the child development books listed in "Suggested Reading" at the back of this book.

Knowing what you want and expect from your child, the next step is to learn how best to bring about that behavior. This is an important way you can increase *your* self-esteem—knowing how to deal with various kinds of behavior and misbehavior. It will also increase self-esteem in your child: Children feel better about themselves when they have confident parents who know how to set rules and bring about compliance with them.

Let's use a practical example to illustrate what I mean.

Suppose you have a five-year-old daughter, and an important value for you as a parent is honesty. You believe that children should be truthful and tell few if any lies. Your five-year-old lied to you about a simple chore. You asked her to feed her kitty. She said she had when she hadn't. She's done this not only once but several times. This certainly violates your sense of what is right.

You have the first part of being a competent parent down pat—you know what you expect (honesty) and what you value (telling the truth). The next part is harder, however. How will you enforce telling the truth and teach her in a way that discourages lying and promotes honesty?

In chapters 8 and 9 are several techniques that could be used to bring about more honest behavior. Asking think questions, telling stories that make a point, and giving praise and rewards are methods you might consider.

Your goal is to change her lying and at the same time not damage her self-esteem. In fact, perhaps you would like to increase her level of self-esteem—even if you use punishment as a technique to handle this problem.

As another example, suppose you expect your children to be kind and sensitive to the feelings of others. Sometimes you see your twelve-year-old acting in a way that is anything but kind and sensitive. How do you handle this?

The discipline techniques in this book are divided into categories based on your goals, so that you can select a category that corresponds with what you are attempting to promote, for instance, chapter 8, "Techniques That Teach Lessons," or chapter 9, "Techniques That Encourage Desired Behavior." Those chapters are intended to give you some ideas about what discipline techniques you could use to bring about those desired goals.

You can sort through the various discipline techniques in each chapter and select one to try based on the situation, the frequency of the problem, the developmental level and personality of your child, and your own inclination.

Let's say that you decide to scold your five-year-old: "Penny, you lied to Mommy and Mommy's tired of this. It's not right to lie and I don't want you to do this any more!"

Was this a right or wrong approach? Did you stop the misbehavior while at the same time increasing Penny's feelings of self-esteem? You may have a better answer when you are done reading this book. For the moment, though, it can be said that scolding and criticism are possible child-discipline techniques that *could* be appropriate and helpful.

It depends on your child and how she reacts to this approach. When you know many kinds of discipline techniques and know when and how to apply them, you will be a calmer, more reasonable, and certainly a more confident parent.

What else do you need to know to get started right as an effective child disciplinarian? Here are a few questions you can ask yourself before you use a discipline technique.

Why Is My Child Acting Like This?

What is causing her behavior? If she is whiny, for instance, is it because she's tired, angry, ill, frustrated? If your son has just stolen an expensive skateboard parked in front of a local store, is it because he lacks moral values, has poor control over his impulses, is trying to get even with the owner of the skateboard, is angry at you, or has a bad habit of stealing?

How you answer these questions (to the best of your ability, because often you will not have a definite answer) determines to some extent which discipline technique you will use. In responding to the misbehavior, you tailor the discipline technique to the reason for the problem. If your daughter is whiny because she is overtired, the best response may be to see she gets a nap or, if that's not possible immediately, to tell her she will feel better when she's gotten some sleep while you try to ignore her whining until she's able to nap.

If your son stole a skateboard to get even with a friend, your approach may be to take away a privilege (see chapter 11) and have a discussion with him about how he could have handled the problem in a more constructive way (see chapter 8).

It is assumed that all misbehavior by children has a cause, and if you can pinpoint or make educated guesses about what that cause is, you will be in a better position to respond to it appropriately.

Some parents use the same technique for each and every misbehavior. Children I see in therapy who have parents like this usually view their parent's customary response as "stupid" and almost always fail to learn anything constructive from discipline that's always the same.

The greatest advantage of this book should be that parents can vary their responses depending on the child, the situation, and the reason for the misbehavior.

What Is My Relationship with My Child?

When you have a close, loving relationship with your child, you will necessarily use a different discipline technique from the one you might select if you have a hostile, conflictual relationship.

If your son Jamal has hit his sister and he already feels you have been picking on him, you will not want to use criticism or spanking. These methods would only increase the emotional distance between you while doing nothing for his self-esteem— except lowering it. On the other hand, if you and Jamal feel warmth and friendliness, you can get away with criticism and a more punitive approach without seriously damaging your relationship. How you feel about each other must be taken into account before you pick a discipline.

In general, when you have a child who does not feel close to you or there is distance and alienation between you, you are better off using the discipline skills in chapter 7 ("Techniques That Foster Self-Control") or chapter 9 ("Techniques That Encourage Desired Behavior").

When a child does feel close to you and wants your approval, you could opt to use the techniques in chapter 8 ("Techniques That Teach Lessons"), chapter 10 ("Techniques That Correct Behavior"), or chapter 11 ("Techniques That Discourage Undesired Behavior").

Are There Other People Present When You Plan to Use a Discipline Method?

Whether other children or adults are present when you discipline your child will make a difference in your approach to discipline.

If fifteen-year-old Sarah is disrespectful to you in front of five of her girlfriends, you may not want to be critical or impose a punishment right then. This is particularly true if Sarah is highly dependent on her friends and their feelings about her. She may lose face and be embarrassed in front of her friends if you say, "Sarah, you're being disrespectful and because of that you can't go to the party tomorrow night."

When Sarah is embarrassed, her self-esteem is wounded and she may become angry at how you treated her in front of her friends. You may have temporarily stopped her disrespectful behavior, but at what cost to your relationship with her, and at what cost to her feelings of self-worth? Could your actions cause greater problems for both of you in the long run? If Sarah were alone with you, or if you waited until her friends went home, you could use the exact same methods with much different results.

Similarly, suppose it's Thanksgiving Day and the whole family is gathered around the dining room table having a sumptuous meal. Your son Sean, a rambunctious nine-year-old, chooses this time to display his worst table manners. He's squirming, spilling food off the edge of his plate, dropping his napkin to the floor, and making strange humming sounds.

You will have to consider carefully how to deal with this problem. For one thing, Sean may admire an older uncle sitting across from him and he would "die" if he were embarrassed in front of this uncle (never mind that he is embarrassing you in front of your whole family!).

Instead of scolding, criticizing, or threatening Sean or removing him from the table for the rest of the meal, you could give him a signal that he is acting inappropriately (see chapter 7). If that fails to bring about more orderly table manners, you may next try asking him to accompany you to the kitchen to "help."

When you're alone in the kitchen, you could use a technique that has a chance of helping him get his table manners under control (see chapter 7).

How Strong Is My Child's Feeling of Self-Esteem?

How children feel about themselves makes a definite difference as to the discipline technique you will use.

Certainly there may be times when a child's level of self-esteem doesn't matter. For instance, when your three-year-old daughter darts into the street, you're not going to sit around trying to figure out how she feels about herself. First you're going to protect her and make sure she's safe. Then you'll deal with her future behavior and teach her a lesson about safety. However, in most other situations, it *will* matter how she feels about herself.

If twelve-year-old Matt feels defeated and thinks everything is going wrong for him, you will not employ a discipline skill that will reinforce the defeated, discouraged feeling. Instead, you will want to offer praise and encouragement for more desired behavior, or focus on his positive behavior rather than his negative behavior.

There are children who are generally compliant and easy to discipline. These are the children about whom parents say, "All you have to do is look at Deidre sideways and she'll cry." With a child like this, you almost never have to take away a privilege or scold. Instead, a mild criticism or disapproving look will let Deidre know what she's doing, and may be all that is needed to bring about a change.

When you have a youngster with good self-esteem, the approach will be different. If Paula usually feels positive about herself, has enthusiasm for life, and achieves well at school and at home, the discipline you use when she skips school will be far different from the one you use with discouraged, low–self-esteem Troy who hates school. You could ground Paula from a dance on Saturday night and know she will tolerate it, accept it, and bounce back by Monday. If Troy were grounded from an important social event, he might well go into an emotional tailspin that would take weeks to reverse.

What Will Happen If I Use This Particular Technique at This Time?

The last and perhaps most important question to ask is how will this discipline technique affect my child. What will be the positive and negative side effects of the use of one or another of the available discipline methods?

Only by studying a whole range of potential responses can you know the usual positive and negative effects of different child-discipline skills and techniques. In the following chapters I will describe nearly every possible discipline technique and the likely responses when you use each of them. Not only will you learn how and when a technique should be used but you will get an idea of good and bad results that can follow.

There are powerful methods you can use to bring about change in the behavior of a child or teenager. But you may choose not to use a specific technique because the side effects may lead to more serious problems.

As an example, consider this: Darrell is not doing his homework for school until late at night. At that point he is tired and grumpy and puts up a fuss. Not only is there conflict with you about completing homework, but he often fails to finish it and then has difficulty getting up for school the next morning because he has stayed up too late.

You can "make" him do his homework by making the punishment very severe. However, the side effects of severe threats or actual loss of privileges could include anger, resentment, and hostility toward you. This is explained in chapter 11. It could also include resistance toward school and failure to turn in homework completed under conditions of extreme threat.

So you could solve the original problem (failure to complete homework in a timely fashion) and in the process create new and more difficult problems. You can use techniques to win the battle, but in so doing lose the war (a good relationship with your child).

When choosing a child discipline technique, both short- and long-term goals must be taken into account.

Punishments can be legitimate methods of discipline in some situations. However, these methods also carry the greatest risks. The side effects can be greater resistance, less communication, and a lowered sense of self-esteem in your child.

By asking and answering the five questions, you are better prepared to choose one of the several techniques discussed in the following chapters.

The idea is not just to stop misbehavior. It is often much more important to increase the behavior you like and improve how your child feels about herself.

Summary

Before using a discipline technique, ask yourself these questions:

- Why is my child acting like this?
- What is my relationship with my child?
- Are there other people present who will observe me using a discipline technique?
- How is my child's self-esteem?
- What will happen if I use a particular discipline technique at this time?

Rules for Parents and Children

MOST PARENTS use rules in haphazard ways.

"Be good," we tell our kids on their way to a birthday party.

"Don't forget to brush your teeth," a child is reminded as he trudges off to bed.

"From now on," we say in exasperation to a daughter who has borrowed her sister's favorite sweater, "leave your sister's clothes alone."

As parents, we often cope with crises with rules ("No more stealing"), or try to promote harmony with new rules ("From now on, each of you has to take turns sitting in the front seat with Dad").

We all have our favorite homilies or moral lessons that we constantly stress: "Honesty is the best policy," "Stay out of trouble," "A good breakfast will get you off to a good start," "Wear your boots when it's raining," "Hang up your clothes as soon as you come in from outdoors," "Never start a fight."

However, very few parents actually view rules as an important part of discipline; few know how to use rules to guide children to do right and to help them change their behavior so that it is more in line with what parents want.

If you are to give rules a proper place among the whole array of discipline techniques, you must understand rules and how to use them effectively. You should be aware of what rules are all about and how successful parents use them.

Why do we have rules in the first place? You know that no organization or society could exist for more than ninety seconds without someone suggesting rules to govern the membership. Children do this in early elementary school when they play marbles, tag, or jump rope ("No red-hot peppers!") or when they form clubs or secret societies ("No boys allowed"). But adults do pretty well for themselves, too. Witness the bylaws of a civic organization or corporation.

What do these rules do for members? They tell them how they are to behave and how they can avoid problems. They are guidelines, limits, and laws to regulate members' behavior. If you know the rules, you feel safer and more secure; if you don't know the rules, you usually feel uncomfortable and disoriented.

Athletes feel the same way. If major league umpires begin enforcing the balk rule for pitchers after not enforcing it for thirty years, pitchers are confused, angry, perhaps even temperamental. If the calls are made consistently by the umpires and the pitchers learn exactly what is expected of them, life becomes safer and more predictable.

So it is for children. They are born into an organization called "the family." Every group has its rules and bylaws and so does each family. As children come to understand the rules and regulations that govern the family, they feel safe, protected, and comfortable.

Rules protect children. They give them a sense of security and ensure a sense of order in their life. If the rules are consistent and reasonable day after day, then children regard their world as predictable. Children certainly need a predictable world. If the rules are changing, uncertain, or fuzzy, children are disoriented and confused and their behavior will reflect this.

Most children do better when their world is structured—when it is well-ordered and the expectations for them are clear. Rules, and the limits indicated by clear rules, suggest the standards and expectations of their parents. Rules such as "We expect you to share your toys," "We want you to treat other people fairly," and "The rule in this house is that if you are under sixteen years old, you must be in the house by 9:30 P.M. every night," are ways of expressing the limits, the structure, and the values of the family. Young people may not always like the rules, but they should always know what we expect.

Start with a Few Simple, Age-Appropriate Rules

Rules given to very young children should be few in number, simple, and related to each child's age and developmental level. Most infants don't need (and can't understand) limits until they become mobile and start walking; that's when they can touch things they're not supposed to and go places they shouldn't.

Until then, what passes for rules tends to be instructions parents hardly expect babies to follow closely. When children begin to sit in a high chair and eat from a spoon and drink from a cup, we'll say "Don't throw your spoon on the floor" after the baby has done exactly that for the fifth time in two minutes, and we can't help but smile because it's cute. Most of us can (and should) be playful and avoid being too serious about rules at this stage; we know that babies are just learning. "Just one more bite and then you'll be all finished," a mother says, scooping the last spoonful of baby food. "Don't spit your food," a father may cajole, well aware that the baby finds it amusing to spit carrots or peas down his chin.

One of the things parents are usually very good about in these early years is giving small children the leeway needed to learn. The rules are not expected to be adhered to in any rigid manner. Later on, though, as children become more capable, the rules take on more formality and more seriousness. Gradually parents begin to expect that the growing child will learn to eat with a fork or a spoon, to chew and swallow food without spitting and dribbling, to use a napkin, to avoid spilling milk, and to stop playing with food.

During the toddler years, as children begin walking and talking and can clearly understand instructions, rules are first explicitly established.

"Don't touch the stove. Hot! It will burn you!" is an early rule. "Don't pull the dog's tail. That hurts him." is another, as is "Don't run into the street. You could be hit by a car!" These rules are expected to make the world safe for children and protect their physical health as well as provide some peace for their parents. How do you best communicate these rules and make them work?

Rules Should Be Clear, Simple, and Understandable

For toddlers and young children, rules should be clear ("Don't draw on the walls"). They should be simple, not complex ("Don't hit others" as opposed to "Other children have rights and you should respect their rights"). And they should be understandable.

Also, it is sometimes effective to pair consequences with a rule so it is clear to children what happens if they violate the rule. For toddlers, rules in the form of rhymes are often very effective. "If you hit, then you must sit!" is easier to remember than "Don't hit other children."

Give Reasons for Rules

It helps children of all ages, but especially preschool children, if the reasons for the rules are given as well. "Don't touch the stove!" may not be as good as "Don't touch the stove because if it is hot it will burn you and that could hurt you very much." Or, "Don't hit other children because it hurts when you hit and it is not fair to make someone else hurt." Children and young people who have good reasoning abilities frequently want (sometimes even demand) to know the reasons for rules.

Be Aware of Your Reasons for Rules

Whether or not you give a reason with every rule, it is important that *you* know the reason for your rule. A rule should be established to provide structure and security in the child's life or to make family life easier and more pleasant. A rule should not be set to satisfy the whim of mother or father or to make the parent's life easy ("Children should be seen and not heard" or "Don't ask so many questions").

Use Consequences to Enforce Rules

How do you best enforce a rule? That depends on the age of your child, on the child's personality, and on the rule. Certainly, there must be consequences if a rule is broken. Those consequences should be reasonable and fair. Consequences that are unfair or unreasonable or that don't seem relevant for a particular offense are likely to cause resentment and hostility rather than compliance with the rule.

Make Rules Realistic

Rules should be within the ability of children to live up to and should take their age into account. For example, it is unrealistic to expect a three-year-old not to cry when he is fatigued or hurt. It may also be very unreasonable to have a rule about getting on the honor roll for a junior high student with severe learning disabilities.

Time Limits Should Be Flexible

Similarly, children must have enough time to carry out a rule. Although the clarity of a rule may be enhanced by placing a time limit on it ("The dishes are to be washed and put away within thirty minutes after dinner is over"), time limits should be flexible; it may **not** really matter, for instance, if the dishes are done thirty minutes or sixty minutes after dinner.

Consequences Should Be Reasonable

Consequences can be given and enforced beginning with toddlers: "If you have a temper tantrum, you must go to your room until you are under control." "If you run into the street, then you must come into the house to play." "If you hit another child, you must sit in a chair for five minutes."

Even at age two or three, children will understand that these are fair and reasonable consequences to the breaking of a rule.

An example of an unreasonable consequence would be slapping or spanking a child because he hit another child or making a child stay in the house for the rest of the day because he did not share a toy in the sandbox. These are overreactions to relatively minor offenses.

Consequences should have something to do with the crime: Major sentences should not be handed down for minor crimes.

Consequences Are Not Always Needed

When a youngster has broken a rule, a consequence is not always needed. Sometimes just reminding the child of the rule and restating it will be sufficient. Also effective is to ask the child what the rule is: "Do you remember what Daddy told you about running in the street? Tell me what Daddy told you before about that."

This technique can be combined with a consequence: "Do you know why Mommy is bringing you in the house to play? Tell me why you have to come in the house now." This not only tests children's knowledge of the rule, but it serves as their own reminder to themselves and helps to increase their compliance with the consequence.

A child who can say, "I ran into the street. That's why I have to go in the house to play," will more than likely go relatively quietly into the house with you.

Elicit Children's Cooperation

Children are more likely to cooperate with rules if there are good reasons given for them, if they are clear, and if they are relatively few in number. If you have a list of fifty rules covering every possible contingency, children are likely to give up on all the rules.

To make sure rules are clear and understood, sometimes it is helpful to ask children to state back the rule and explain what it means to them.

Another way to help bring about cooperation is to give children a chance to participate in the making of a rule. "Both you and your brother complain all the time about who gets to watch what on television. What do you think would be a good rule we could use to help decide who gets to watch what program?" This kind of discussion is more likely to lead to an agreed-upon rule than an autocratic rule laid down by the parent: "I've decided that from now on *I* will decide which program we will watch."

For some families, it is then helpful to post the rule on the refrigerator or in another conspicuous spot. This serves as a reminder that a rule exists and remains in force.

Expect Children to Test Rules

Part of your expectation as a parent should be that children will disobey or test rules. As learners, children need a little leeway. They need to be given the opportunity to try out rules and push the limits.

Children test rules and limits because their own controls aren't well established and because they need to know that someone else will protect them from their own impulses. As a parent, your job is to expect that testing of the rules will occur and then be strong enough to make the rules and the limits clear. Consistent and firm rules are a safety net for children. They test them from time to time to be assured that the safety net is there.

Stephen was a ten-year-old boy I saw in treatment. He frequently tested rules. One day he was angry with his mother because she wouldn't buy him a game when they were shopping. He harassed her as they began the trip home, calling her "cheap." She allowed this with little response until Stephen increased the verbal assault. When he called her a witch and put his muddy shoes on the dashboard of the car, she could no longer tolerate his pushing the limits. She told him he was grounded, restricted to the house for the rest of the day and not allowed to use the phone. Stephen not only accepted the punishment but stopped berating his mother. Her response was a safety net to stop Stephen when his own controls were not working well.

Children Need Reminders of the Rules

With little children, frequent reminders about rules are necessary. "Now remember, let Mommy know if you are going to Billy's house to play." Expect young children to forget these kinds of rules occasionally.

Older children may need not merely a reminder but a more serious consequence. A twelve-year-old boy who has played his stereo too loud after 10:00 P.M. may have to forfeit the privilege of playing the stereo for three days. A ten-year-old girl who was caught shoplifting may have to forfeit her allowance for one month and reimburse the store.

But no matter how old the child, there should be a reminder of what the rule is and the reason behind it. This serves to reinforce the family standards and values and to indicate how important they are to you. And it is important to keep in mind that just because children forget and test rules does not mean a rule is not working or needs to be revised. Nor does it mean that punishments or consequences are needed to bring about quicker compliance. Rules do not have to be learned or complied with forever. Just remember that children—even at sixteen and seventeen years old—are learners and students of life. We do not have to expect them to be perfect or to always remember the rules. They will make mistakes and that is why rule reminders are important.

Some Rules May Have to Be Changed

There are times, though, when a rule turns out to be bad, or proves unenforceable, or plainly doesn't work. Fourteen-year-old Danny provides an illustration.

Danny had been smoking for one year before his parents discovered that he went through about a pack of cigarettes a week. When they found out, they instantly made a rule: No cigarettes and no smoking on our property. Even so, Danny's father often saw a pack of cigarettes in Danny's shirt pocket or found a recently smoked butt behind the garage. Danny never denied it when he was caught but he kept doing it.

As the consequences and punishments were increased, there was no change in his behavior; Danny continued to bring cigarettes on the property. Since he wasn't smoking in the house, his parents finally decided their rule about no smoking and no cigarettes on the property wasn't enforceable. They decided to talk with Danny. The result of this discussion was a new attempt at formulating a rule that would work.

Danny suggested the following new rule: "I won't smoke in the house and I won't even bring cigarettes in the house as long as I can smoke outside if I'm careful and make sure every cigarette is out and not burning when I'm done." His parents agreed and Danny then stuck to the new rule. His smoking became an open topic between them all and no longer a secret; Danny felt much better because he didn't have to sneak around any more. (There are other issues involved here—that smoking is bad for his health and that his parents are still opposed to smoking in general, for instance; for other discipline techniques to handle those issues, consider the skills discussed in chapters 7, 8, and 9.)

Parents Need to Follow Rules, Too

Another point should be made about children's cooperation and compliance with rules—this has to do with exceptions to rules and hypocrisy. As children get older, and particularly when they are preadolescents and adolescents, they are acutely aware of the unequal application of rules. If you enforce a rule for one child and ignore a violation of the same rule for another child, you've got some potentially serious rebellion on your hands. It doesn't matter how good the rule is. If it is not equally applied to all, it may not work.

The same thing holds true for parents and their own compliance with family rules. If you make a rule, then you should be willing to follow it. I know parents who smoke and yet have a rule about no smoking in the house. They have considerable difficulty winning cooperation from their children for this kind of rule because they don't follow it themselves.

Curfew rules often give rise to this kind of conflict. While children and teenagers can understand that parents are allowed to stay out later than their children, they may not be so cooperative if you violate the spirit of the rule. The spirit of most curfew rules goes something like this: "As parents, we get very worried when you're out too late. Often we can't sleep. So to allow us to get enough sleep and not have to worry about you, you must be home by eleven o'clock." Now, that part's fine.

But what about when one or both parents repeatedly go out and don't let the children know when they're returning? Is it any more fair for a child to have to worry about his parents than for a parent to worry about a child? I think not. And I do know that children worry about such things.

I know a seventeen-year-old girl who is questioning her mother's rule about sexual intercourse before marriage. This is a bright, sensitive, and articulate girl who was raised with her mother's rule "You should save yourself for the man you are going to marry." Which was fine until her mother divorced and started dating.

A month into a new relationship with a man, her mother announced to seventeen-year-old Debbie that she was going out of town for a weekend with her new boyfriend. "I don't think that's right," said Debbie. "Why does one rule apply to me and one apply to her?"

When she confronted her mother about this, her mother told her that *she* was the parent and *she* could do what she wanted. Within one month after this confrontation, Debbie scheduled an appointment with the family doctor to get birth control pills. There had been too much hypocrisy in the following of this particular rule for Debbie to handle.

Firm Enforcement of Rules Is Essential

Children are more likely to cooperate with rules if there are not too many exceptions to them. The rules have to be flexible, but that flexibility cannot be interpreted as softness, permissiveness, and a lack of resolve to do something if the rule is violated.

Children, especially teenagers, will test rules if they have come to believe the rules will not be enforced. This was true with Jill, a sixteen-year-old girl I knew who seemed more interested in rock music than in school.

Jill's parents were divorced and both wanted to see her do well in school. Yet there were frequent disagreements between her parents over the enforcement of rules. Her father often thought her mother was too strict and harsh, while her mother thought Jill's father was too permissive and unwilling to enforce rules. Jill tended to play them against each other.

The showdown came when Jill had tickets to a Van Halen concert. Two days before the big evening, Jill skipped school. When her mother found out, Jill was grounded for the weekend, and that meant she would not be able to go to the concert.

She went to her father and pleaded with him to intervene with her mother. "Why don't you let me stay at your house this weekend," she said, "and then you could let me go to the concert. I'll stay in next weekend."

This time, however, her father decided that the grounding was fair. He refused. Jill thought that if she stuck to her intentions of going to the concert one or both of her parents would give in. She said, "I don't care if I'm grounded or not; I'm going to Van Halen."

"If you go," both parents agreed, "you'll be grounded not for just this weekend, but for three more weekends." Jill had not had to face both parents like this. But the battlelines were drawn. She could give in and let her parents win, or she could go and see what happened.

The result? Jill went to the concert. Her parents talked and agreed she would be grounded for three more weekends and that applied no matter where she was spending the weekend. Furthermore, they also agreed that Jill was getting out of hand if she was defying both parents and pledged to stick together even if they didn't always see eye-to-eye about discipline. The long-term result was that Jill never again violated a stated rule.

Firmness means you are willing to back up a rule with a consequence or a punishment. It means no matter how much complaining or crying you hear, you are sure that you are right about the rule, and if it is violated, there will be a negative consequence.

As CHILDREN BECOME teenagers, rules to regulate their behavior when they are out of your sight become unenforceable. You can't very well enforce any rule about their friendships, their behavior at school, or their actions in a store with friends. You can tell them what you expect, you can enforce broken rules when they are brought to your attention, and you can hope for cooperation.

By the time children are teenagers, you have to trust that your earlier rules, your consistency, clarity, firmness, and fairness have produced the ultimate result: a child who knows what the limits are and has learned self-discipline.

In the beginning, we give children the rules and enforce them. As they become teenagers and move toward adulthood, if we have done our job, they should be able to put rules and limits on their own behavior.

That, after all, is the highest tribute for parents: Our children are self-disciplined individuals who understand that living in society means following rules.

Summary

Remember, rules are more effective if:

- You start with a few simple, age-appropriate rules.
- Rules are clear, simple, and understandable.
- You give reasons for rules.
- You use reasonable consequences to enforce rules.
- You make rules realistic.
- Time limits are flexible.
- You elicit children's cooperation.
- You expect children to test rules.
- You remind children frequently of the rules.
- You change rules as needed.
- You follow rules, too.
- You firmly enforce rules.

FIVE

First Discipline: Techniques That Prevent Early Problems

AROUND THE END of the first year or between the first and second year, children begin walking, putting words together to form sentences, and understanding more of what we're saying. That's usually when parents feel more comfortable giving their children direction and correction and when discipline starts.

It is very important for parents to begin to guide their children for their own protection—not the parent's, the child's. There are too many things children can get into at this stage, too many ways they can hurt themselves as they explore the world of their house or yard.

First discipline from parents is aimed at teaching children how to protect themselves and how to be a member of the family. The discipline and management techniques parents will use with toddlers, therefore, involve socialization and self-protection.

Setting limits and teaching rules are vital to helping socialize children so they live without conflict at home and elsewhere. Therefore, the first discipline technique parents will use with young children is to teach limits.

1. Teach Limits

In teaching limits and letting children know about the rules of the family, it is important that parents combine words with quick action. If a child is about to do something dangerous, a mother or father must swiftly say, "Don't touch the knife! Sharp. Cut!" Maybe the child doesn't understand the concept of cut yet, but a child will understand that when you spring into action and say the rule (don't touch sharp knives), you are conveying something you believe is important.

As young children explore new areas of the house they are now able to reach, like countertops and tabletops, you will need to give them new rules.

Limits in the kitchen may be: children cannot touch knives, must ask to pour a glass of milk, and must not turn on the microwave.

In the bathroom, you may allow the child to turn on the faucet to get a drink in a plastic cup, but not to turn on the hot water for a bath or shower, and certainly not to throw toys in the toilet.

It is important to verbalize these limits often: "No, you cannot play at your friend's house without asking Mommy's permission." And frequently it will be necessary to back up the limits with a statement of consequences. ("If you mark on the wall with crayons, then you must sit on the chair.") Appropriate consequences are discussed later.

If you teach these limits well by stating them often, making them clear and unambiguous, and backing them up with consistent and fair consequences, they will be invaluable for children and help avoid further problems.

Diane, the thirty-year-old mother of a very active two-year-old, brought her son to me and told me, "Jimmy can destroy a room in a few minutes." Jimmy would go from one no-no to another in a seemingly random pattern—pulling books off shelves, eating crayons, pulling plants out of their pots, and attempting to push Diane out of her chair so he could sit in it.

Diane's task was to teach Jimmy limits. That meant that she needed to spend considerable time with Jimmy to keep him safe and any room relatively intact. In teaching the limits Jimmy had never learned, Diane was instructed to tell him, "No. You cannot touch the plants" or "Crayons are for coloring on paper, not for eating." She was then to demonstrate proper behavior by, for instance, showing how to color on a piece of paper. She was also to use if-then statements. "If you eat the crayons, then I will take them away from you."

Just being told this was reassuring to Diane, since she had begun to think that she had an emotionally disturbed child who might never learn to follow rules and obey limits. But with her consistent effort, Jimmy was heeding limits within three months.

2. Use Distraction

This is a technique almost all parents of young children have used, because it works so well. When your two-year-old is trying to operate the VCR or the CD player, try distraction: "Leave Daddy's CD player alone, honey, let's color instead."

Taking the child by the hand to the coloring book and crayons, in most cases will sufficiently divert her attention to this other, equally appealing, activity.

When two-and-a-half-year-old Amanda insists on going to the refrigerator and asking for Popsicles, distract her with something else she would like. "Let's look at the new book

Grandma brought you. It has pictures of animals in it."

Jimmy's mother, Diane, now uses distractions as well as nos. She carries a small Hot Wheels car in her purse so that when Jimmy is beginning to bother strangers in a doctor's office, for example, Diane can reach in her purse and show him the bright red car he enjoys. When he's taking a bath and splashing too much water out of the tub, Diane has a basket of his favorite rubber and plastic toys on hand to redirect his attention.

Distraction can be used with older children, but is most effective with children in the preschool years. Some very determined tots will not be easily distracted, however.

3. Offer Substitutes

Offering substitutes is a useful technique that works very well with young children—and offers an overwhelmed mother or father a change from constantly having to say "No!" or "Don't!" By using a substitute activity, you also teach acceptable alternatives.

When young Mandy is playing with the knobs on the TV, for instance, you can say to her: "I'm going to read a story to some lucky, pretty little girl in this room. Do you know who that might be?" That not only helps make a game of discipline (the next technique to be discussed), but gives Mandy an alternative that is not annoying or against the rules.

Reading a story to Mandy or having her color teaches her not only what she is not supposed to do, but also what she is allowed and encouraged to do. By doing the activity with her (reading to her or coloring with her), you are demonstrating approved and desired alternative behavior.

Other acceptable substitutes for young children might include a favorate cartoon video or a children's television program to watch, a colorful picture book to look at, or a brightly colored Nerf ball, plastic dishes, or a soft, furry handpuppet to play with.

By offering substitutes, in effect you are saying, "I would rather you played with your doll than stand by the new baby's crib touching her ears." But you're doing this without saying it, without criticizing the child, and without telling her she's doing something wrong.

4. Make a Game of Discipline

Making a game out of things is as important a discipline technique as you are likely to use in the early years. There are lots of things you want your child to do, but you certainly can't lecture an eighteen-month-old child on the importance of following the rules about eating properly. You can make mealtime fun, though, by making a game of eating (particularly the icky-tasting foods that children seem to universally dislike).

When you want to begin teaching a two- or three-year-old about the importance of picking up toys and clothes, making a game or a competition of it usually works wonders. "Let's see who can pick up the most blocks" or "I bet I can throw more toys in the toy box than you" will get the interest and ensure the participation of most children—even if it is for only a few seconds or three blocks. At least it's a start toward a lifetime of more orderly habits. You can worry about how to teach a youngster to pick up toys and put them away at another time.

With this discipline technique you are accomplishing an immediate objective and avoiding a more serious confrontation. A real confrontation between you could turn into a battle of wills that would be unproductive and fail to teach the youngster anything important.

Confrontations, unfortunately, are a typical problem. I recall seeing a man and his two- or three-year-old walking down a hall in a public building. The tyke insisted on going in the opposite direction. The man started off kindly enough, but as the youngster resisted going in the right direction, his father became more insistant, finally dragging the now crying child by the arm. All the man had to do was suggest that they race to the end of the hall and the problem would have been resolved far more pleasantly.

Here are some other ways of making a game of discipline. When eating vegetables is a concern, suggest that there is going to be a contest to see who eats five green beans first. The winner gets a prize. Children who dawdle when putting on their shoes and socks might be engaged in some fantasy play: "Let's pretend there's this giant crocodile that nibbles on children's bare feet. Children who are quick about putting on their shoes and socks never get their toes nibbled. Okay, ready? Here comes the crocodile. His mouth is open, see those sharp teeth? Hurry up! He's getting closer! Wow! You finished just in time! That was close."

5. Limit Access to Objects and Activities

If you want to avoid having to pick up too many toys, then you should limit access to objects and activities.

This can mean having your child put some toys away before she begins to play with others or putting some toys out of her sight so that she has only a limited number of toys at any one time. It can also mean limiting a child's access to toys that are meant for older children, that she may not be ready for, or that cause too much frustration.

This last point is important. Children should not be given toys or games that are beyond their interest level or cause them too much frustration. It is the parent's role to help children feel secure and like themselves. A game that is beyond a child's ability, like a puzzle intended for a six-year-old that a three-year-old is struggling with, should be put away for a couple of years. Give the child something more suited to her own age level that will keep her happily and busily engaged.

Limiting access to objects or activities can mean not allowing your child to play with older children who are too mean or rough. It could also mean limiting play or activities that are too stimulating, particularly just before bedtime, or too dangerous, like playing with sharp scissors.

6. Childproof Your Home

Childproofing a home means removing seductive objects or temptations that may attract your young child instead of yelling "No!" Children need to be protected from their own impulses and underdeveloped set of controls. Take that $165 crystal vase off the coffee table until the child is less likely to want to play with every object that reflects light; store breakable objects until children are old enough to understand what is off limits to touch.

The following happened to a good and attentive mother. It was nearing Christmas and she wanted to make the home festive. As part of her holiday decorations, she put candles around. Her nineteen-month-old daughter, an active, smart girl, was fascinated by all the bright and cheery decorations.

One evening the mother lit the candles, which increased the wonderful atmosphere of the house. Just as she was teaching her daughter about the dangers of candles and how a candle flame could burn her if she touched it, guests arrived. It took only a few seconds, but when mother returned from answering the door, she found Kellie backed into a corner with a frightened look on her face saying "I didn't mean it, Mama." On the floor by the candle was a burning dinner napkin and a little plume of rising smoke. Kellie's mother quickly put out the fire and sent Kellie to her room. But she knew that she was probably more to blame for this incident than Kellie. She had not childproofed her home and was expecting more of Kellie than was reasonable under the circumstances.

Removing seductive objects is important in preventing long-range problems; a child deserves not to spend her first three or four years being shouted at because she is attracted to wonderful-looking things. (If you didn't think it looked wonderful, you wouldn't use it or have purchased it in the first place!)

Children also need to be protected from their ineptitude or clumsiness. Because their motor skills are not well developed at first, they drop things, spill things, and unsuccessfully reach for things. That's why most parents provide their children with covered mugs at first instead of actual glasses. This concept should be continued throughout childhood. For instance, putting a plastic covering over the carpet under a child's chair at mealtimes will protect both the carpet and the child's feelings of competence.

Childproofing also means removing items that could be dangerous to children and placing them behind locked doors. Since children are curious, they explore beneath sinks, in cupboards, and in basements and garages. Poisons, detergents, solvents, kerosene, gasoline, and other such things should be out of the way of curious children. If you do your job of protecting children, you save yourself and your child from a behavior problem (and perhaps from a dangerous accident).

7. Criticize the Behavior, Not the Child

A technique that helps prevent later problems is criticizing the behavior, not the child. A child is not bad because she wants to see if a dinner napkin will burn. She may be a very bright and curious child, but that doesn't mean the behavior isn't dangerous.

Much of children's early exploratory behavior can be dangerous. The results of the behavior are the problem, not the child or the child's personality traits.

To be sure the emphasis is in the right place, you can say: "Running into the street is very dangerous and you could be hurt! That would make Mommy very sad. I know you don't want to be hurt." Or, "Hitting hurts your brother. Don't hit!"

Never say: "You're a bad boy! Mommy told you never to leave the yard and you never listen to Mommy!"

Other *don'ts* that attack the child rather than the behavior are:

- "You are too irresponsible."
- "When are you going to grow up and use some sense?"
- "You're a stubborn, willful child!"

A child's self-esteem is too important and her self-image too fragile at this age. There should be no confusion about what you don't like; make it clear you don't like the behavior, while you still love the child.

8. Repeat Rules Often

Young children need to have rules repeated often. There are many rules in life for youngsters to learn, and it is easy to forget them.

Because a child forgets a rule doesn't mean she is evil, spiteful, rebellious, or destined for a life of delinquency. All it means is that a rule was temporarily forgotten. Your job is to be sure your children are reminded of the rules, that they learn the major rules of life and the family over time (from birth to age sixteen or eighteen), and that they remember them at the right times.

Stating a rule once does not guarantee that children will

remember or obey it. Sometimes they will be distracted in play and forget all about your rules. If a group of neighborhood children are laughing and playing in the backyard and one child suggests going over to play on the swing set in another child's yard, four-year-old Ashley may forget that she's supposed to ask her mother before she leaves her yard. Another child may be too impulsive to remember the rule. Another child may need approval so badly from playmates that rules fly away when they should be remembered.

If you understand your child, then you can respond appropriately.

9. Use Rhyming Rules

Rhyming rules (if you hit, then you must sit; stop, look, and listen before you cross the street, always use your eyes before you use your feet) are appealing to children because they can remember them and they make sense.

Children are more likely to repeat these rules to themselves when they need them. Most adults still remember rules, rhyming or otherwise, that they learned as a youngster.

Other examples of rhyming rules are:

- Sassy boys don't play with toys.
- Disobey and you have to stay [in the house].
- Tell a lie and say goodbye.
- A fight's not right.

10. Avoid Abrupt Changes

Nothing is more sure to bring about a temper tantrum or a showdown between parent and child than a mother or father suddenly announcing: "Time for bed" or "Stop that right now!"

Instead, avoid an abrupt change or command by using a preview or warning. Most children react much better if given a warning: "Most of the good children in this house will be safe in their warm beds in fifteen minutes."

"Now hear this, my wonderful child! At the next commercial, children will be putting their pajamas on and heading to bed!" The warning can be given a few times, so by the time zero hour arrives there is no surprise and probably no tantrum or scene—the child has been warned.

Most children need an adjustment period at a time of transition. They cannot be ordered around ("Stop coloring now, it is time for lunch") and expected to respond like robots.

11. Offer Help Through Frustrating Situations

Another way parents can protect children and prevent problems is by offering help in frustrating situations. Don't let a child founder helplessly with a problem.

For example, suppose your son wants to dress himself, but puts both feet in the same pants leg. That's when your help is needed, before a bad mood sets in.

Or suppose your daughter wants to construct a Lego building but has a hard time fitting pieces together accurately. Give her a little help with the difficult parts without taking over or making her feel inadequate.

Toddlers and preschoolers spread their fledgling wings to try many things. It is typical for them to say "I can do it" to a parent offering assistance, then become frustrated and give up when they are not successful. On the other hand, if a parent takes over and does it for them, they can become dependent.

Instead of doing the task entirely for the child, give her some assistance through the frustrating part and then let her do the rest.

You could say, "Ah ha, there's a problem here. Let's try this way and see if it works." Or, "Putting on jackets is difficult. I think if you try this sleeve like this you can do it all by yourself."

12. Anticipate and Avert Problems

Anticipatory planning is another first discipline technique that can prevent problems and keep a parent's nerves from fraying. By planning ahead and preparing a child for an event that might be ripe for problems you can avert a disaster before it occurs.

Without anticipatory planning and careful thought by the parent, a child can be cranky and ornery on a long automobile trip. You can prepare for a car trip by selecting some interesting toys or activities to take along that will keep your child occupied. They might include small toys, dolls or stuffed animals, and books.

Similarly, children at a restaurant that caters to adults will be bored and restless as they wait for some food. Parents can make a trip to a restaurant more enjoyable by letting children know what to expect and how to behave, discussing the menu ahead of time, and bringing puzzles, books, and drawing materials to keep children from becoming bored.

Before going to a store, you might say to your child, "In the store we're going to, children are not allowed to touch things on the shelves. So I won't be able to let you touch anything. But you can pick out a toy to take with you to hold while we go through the store."

If you are taking your child to the supermarket, select a store that has children's carts and let your youngster push her own cart and help you shop. If there are no children's carts, give your child a manageable list of items to find for you.

I can recall taking my own children to the theater and to concerts when they were two and three years old. I expected them to sit quietly and appreciate the wonderful culture they were being exposed to. Things worked much better, I discovered—there was less rustling of programs and restlessness—when they were allowed to take a book to read (if it was light enough in the theater) if they got bored or a hand puzzle to work.

13. Offer Choices

When problems do develop in a store, theater, restaurant, or at home, children will respond better if you give them choices rather than make demands.

Instead of saying "Get over here this instant" when your child wanders away in the grocery store, you'll generally be more successful if you say "Would you rather walk by Mommy or ride in the cart?"

When a child is being too clingy, you can ask: "Do you wish to play in your room with your doll or outside with Melissa?"

Before your daughter's afternoon nap you can give her a choice: "Do you want a glass of juice now or after your nap?"

A child who is resisting bedtime can be given this choice: "Would you like me to read *Green Eggs and Ham* or *Cinderella* when you're tucked in bed?"

If children know through experience that you mean business and will follow through, they will make a choice and go along with it. But you should not expect instant compliance. Give them an opportunity to think about the choices you offer and come to a decision. Let them know that you will make the choice for them if they don't do it on their own.

It's important not to give more than two choices to young children. If you offer three or more alternatives ("You can wear your blue jeans, your dress, or your leotard"), it's usually too much for them to handle.

Choices for young children work well at mealtime, when it's time to get dressed, at playtime ("Do you want to play outside or use watercolors on the kitchen counter?"), and at bedtime—all times when there are potential discipline challenges.

14. Give Leeway to Make Mistakes

Give children some leeway to make mistakes. This can be called learner's leeway.

When children are learning to walk, they are expected to fall down. Likewise, in other situations, children cannot be expected to make the transition to new behavior without some setbacks and errors. Children who are learning to put on their shoes sometimes put them on the wrong feet. When they are dressing themselves, they may put on mismatched clothes. In learning to drink from a glass, they will inevitably spill milk.

Giving children the opportunity to make mistakes is one of the prices we pay in order to let them try new behavior. If you are encouraging growth and development, then you accept that children will try and fail. By giving them leeway, you are exempting them from punishment and criticism for any failures or mistakes.

To give them leeway, you need to be tolerant, patient, understanding, and accepting of the things that go wrong as children develop. There are times when they will test limits, forget rules, and occasionally "screw up." That's what all learners do.

Summary

First discipline techniques to be used with children eighteen months to thirty-six months of age to help prevent later problems include:

- Teach limits.
- Use distraction.
- Offer substitutes.
- Make a game of discipline.
- Limit access to objects and activities.
- Childproof your home.
- Criticize the behavior, not the child.
- Repeat rules often.
- Use rhyming rules.
- Avoid abrupt changes.
- Offer help through frustrating situations.
- Anticipate and avert problems.
- Offer choices.
- Give leeway to make mistakes.

S I X

Techniques That Prevent Later Problems

FEW SUBJECTS generate as much concern among parents as discipline. Whenever parents get together, eventually the discussion comes around to discipline and how various behavior problems are handled—or mishandled.

I like to think of discipline as a way to guide children in the right direction. The right direction is one that leads children to be self-disciplined.

In order to guide children to that point, though, mothers and fathers have to help them build up their controls, just as parents help children grow healthy bodies by seeing that they eat the right foods and get proper exercise. Feeding kids right, though, doesn't mean they will never indulge in cookies, hamburgers, and french fries. Why? Because it's impractical to insist they eat only proper foods. You could try, but you wouldn't have a very happy relationship with your children. They would be angry and see you as unreasonable if they couldn't occasionally eat at McDonald's or Burger King like all the other kids (whose parents also worry about them eating the right foods).

So it is with discipline. As much as you want your children to learn to follow your rules and stay within the limits you set, you can't always insist that they always toe the mark and never break a rule. It's more realistic to hope that as little beginners in life they will gradually learn to stick to the guidelines you've established at home, at school, and on the playground.

You can give children a head start with developing self-control by taking preventive action. With older children, just as with toddlers, there are discipline techniques that help to prevent problems before they occur.

Most children are normal, but as immature individuals they are likely to use poor judgment and immature thinking or reasoning skills. The techniques in this chapter allow you to take positive action before a problem begins rather than waiting for bad behavior. Since you are dealing with a child, unsophisticated in the ways of the world (really, this is true, even if it doesn't always seem so!), you must do the thinking and the preplanning to avert problems.

Preventive discipline can take many forms at various ages. In nine-year-old Brad's family, the children were encouraged to participate in sports, but Brad's mother was well aware of his sensitivity to criticism and low self-esteem. On the way to a baseball game in which Brad was to play, his mother listened closely to his comments, which suggested that he was worried about the game, his own playing ability, and the recent decisions of the coach about who would regularly play his position.

She also knew that the coach tended to be abrupt in his decisions and to give orders to the boys on the team without adequate explanations. When Brad was busy warming up, catching fly balls in the outfield, she asked the coach for a minute of his time. "When you take Brad out of the game today, do me a favor," she began. "Will you give him some words of encouragement and let him know the exact reason you're taking him out of the game?"

The coach agreed. In the fifth inning, when Brad was replaced at his second-base position, the coach took Brad aside and complied with the agreement with Brad's mother. Brad was pleased with the positive words he heard from the coach and on the way home his mother was very much aware that Brad felt good about his performance and was not focusing on being removed from the game.

In another family, seventeen-year-old Jason had asked permission to use the family car on Saturday night to drive to his soccer game. On Saturday morning, however, a snowstorm dumped four inches of snow on the city. Jason was told that it could become too dangerous for him to drive.

Despite Jason's pleas and promises to drive carefully, his parents conferred throughout the day, and two hours before the game they made their decision: Jason could not drive. He was initially angry and accused his parents of a lack of trust in his ability. Their decision, however, was firm, and Jason found another way to the game. His parents had prevented a possible accident with their decision; if an accident had occurred, the results would have had more far-reaching consequences than Jason's temporary hurt feelings.

That is what this chapter is all about—preplanning and preventive thinking by parents to avoid problems before they occur.

1. Offer Choices

We offer choices to toddlers, but they are also useful at later ages, even into the teen years. Choices still work and should be used to assist kids of all ages to avoid greater problems.

As an example, think of an eleven-year-old who has been invited with his parents to a party where there are only adults.

You know if he attends this party he is likely to become bored and to look for attention. He will attempt to be involved in adult conversations or adult games. This will bother you as you try to keep him from annoying others at the party.

Instead of allowing potential discipline problems to evolve, use a choice: "Mark, you've got two choices. You can go to the Jones's party and take two books or games you enjoy, or you can stay overnight at your grandmother's house. It's your decision."

Or another example: If a teenager is insisting on going to a concert after you've grounded him, you could try to use force to prevent him from going—and risk a much greater problem, perhaps even a physical tussle. Or you can offer choices, hoping to avoid more difficulty by giving him a chance to use good judgment: "You have a decision to make. We have already said you're grounded. You can accept your grounding and stay home or you can attend the concert. We can't stop that. If you go to the concert, you will be grounded longer and we will be disappointed in you, but it is up to you to make the final decision."

At a rodeo, nine-year-old Ryan was annoying his friend Jack, whom he and his mother had invited. Ryan's mother leaned over to Ryan and whispered: "You have a choice: Switch seats with me or you can sit in the car for the rest of the show."

When elementary school siblings are arguing about who gets to sit in the front seat with Mom, they can be given a choice: "You can make up a rule that allows you to take turns about who sits in the front seat, or you can both sit in the back seat."

2. Give Rule Reminders

Children of all ages need rule reminders. Just as three- and four-year-olds need to be reminded of rules, so do older children and teenagers. And not only do rules need reiteration, but so do the parents' values. It's easy for kids to forget about rules in the excitement of being with other children or in social situations like parties, group play, or games.

Children and teens with impulsive problems (such as Attention Deficit Hyperactivity Disorder) have particular difficulty remembering what the rules are. What they need from their parents, even if they sometimes resent hearing it, are reminders that draw their attention to a rule and a potential problem.

Rule reminders are particularly important at crucial times, as in the following examples.

Four-year-old Ben is getting ready to go to his day-care center for the day. As she kisses him goodbye, his mother says, "Don't forget our rule, Ben. Four-year-olds don't bite other children." To which Ben replies, "Okay, Mom." And he will remember this rule. Maybe not all day, but the more it is repeated to him, the easier it will be for him to remember when another child is irritating him and he is about to bite out of frustration and anger.

Eight-year-old Tammy is about to leave for a birthday party. Her father reminds her: "Remember, dear, stay there until I come to pick you up. Don't try to walk home by yourself."

Parents can remind children of rules in various ways. They can ask as questions: "Do you remember what you're going to do at school today if you start to have a temper tantrum?" Or they can jog the memory: "Don't forget the rule."

Usually it's the repetition of the rule that in the long run will cause it to spring to mind when children most need it.

3. Establish a Routine

Establish a routine to help keep kids out of trouble. Children sometimes misbehave because they don't know what to do or what is expected of them. You can solve this by developing a routine or ritual that gives them something to do at critical times.

One of the most difficult times for many mothers, whether they work or not, is just before dinner, when they are busy in the kitchen preparing supper. Obviously, this can apply to fathers who are responsible for cooking dinner. Children tend to look for attention and want to be closer to their parent then, either because they need attention or want to be where the action is. What can you do to keep them out of your way while you prepare dinner? You can scold them, punish them, or take some preventive action.

To take preventive action, establish a routine for this time of the evening. If the child is old enough, you can have him assist you with a specific set of chores during meal preparation. If the child is too young, the routine could involve having specific playthings—plastic dishes, for instance—in the kitchen or establishing a game that the child plays every evening at this time. The routine is established when you say that this will be "our time" or "your time" to assist Dad or Mom. Then, make this consistently so.

Suppose you have a seven-year-old who interrupts you whenever you're on the telephone. It's easy to yell at the child or scold him while you're on the phone and afterward. A better approach is to establish a routine that deals with this problem.

"Here's what we're going to do whenever I'm talking on the phone. We will put a hobby box by the phone. Whenever I'm talking on the phone, you may come to the hobby box and cut, paste, or draw. That will be what you do so you are not tempted to interrupt me while I'm talking on the phone."

Think about the times of day and the various situations in which you encounter similar problems with your child, and establish a routine that will prevent the problem.

4. Remove Seductive Objects

Children of all ages also need relief from certain temptations. Removing seductive objects works as well for older children and teens as it does for toddlers.

Instead of arguing with a high school student about whether he is studying too little and watching television too much, remove the TV from his bedroom or the place where he normally studies. Take a squirt gun away from that nine-year-old girl who, if given a few minutes with the toy in her possession, would fire the initial watery salvos in an all-out, in-house water fight with her brother.

Before leaving a twelve-year-old with his older sister for the weekend, don't just tell him he can't ride his BMX racer in your absence. If you really want to remove the temptation, be sure to take the key to the shed housing the bike.

5. Plan in Advance

Most children, regardless of age, need some sort of advance planning at times. They don't always know how to anticipate problems. Or, in their excitement to do something, they don't consider all the potential problems or drawbacks. They frequently need assistance to anticipate consequences.

Here, again, is where you as the adult can do some anticipatory planning to head off a problem before it begins. How you use this discipline technique depends on knowing your own child and imagining what is likely to go wrong, and then taking appropriate action beforehand to avoid the most likely problems.

If you are planning to take a five-year-old to a restaurant, you might tell him before you leave home what to expect and what kind of restaurant it is. Then, help him pick out one item to take along to avoid boredom or the temptation to misbehave.

If Sandy, who typically becomes overexcited in many situations, is scheduled to go with her second-grade class to a circus, advance planning will be important. Give her an idea what to expect and how you would like her to handle herself. Let her know how stimulating a circus can be. Suggest she pick out one ring to watch at a time rather than try to take in all the activities at once. In this situation, advance planning with her teacher (the brave soul who has volunteered to take twenty-four second-graders to the circus) might be valuable. Some hints on how the teacher can best handle Sandy when she is overstimulated could be helpful to him.

As kids get older, if you teach them to think ahead about what some of the difficulties are likely to be in various situations, they will begin to do this on their own. In the early years you will do this for them and even make strong suggestions about ways they can plan to avoid serious behavior problems.

6. Define Limits

It is often helpful to define the limits for children every so often. Defining the limits means letting kids know where the boundaries are and where your patience and tolerance ends. This does not imply that enforcement is an issue; it just means that children are told what the limits are.

Kathy, a thirteen-year-old, often had things like this to say: "Boy, is my language arts teacher ever dumb! Do you know that he gave me a pass to the library today during second hour and he forgot that the library was closed? I had a whole hour to walk around the halls and try to get my friends out of their classes."

For kids like Kathy, limits are critical. If she can get away with something that makes adults look stupid, she will. When limits are imposed, however, she may still complain, but she generally goes along with them. What she requires is a teacher or parent who says, "You're not getting a pass because I know the library is closed. Instead, I expect you to stay right here and finish your assignment. You cannot walk around the halls causing trouble."

When fourteen-year-old Richie wanted to go to an Iron Maiden concert with some friends, he lined up a ride with a nineteen-year-old friend and found a source for tickets. He waited until the night before the concert and then sprang it on his mother and stepfather. Naturally, they asked who he was going with. When he told them, their response was: "Wally? No way! He's been in two accidents already when he was drinking. We think too much of you to let you go out in a car with him. Besides that, you should have told us about this before tonight. Sorry, but it looks like you're not going to this concert."

Richie may have been disappointed and angry with both his mother and stepfather, but he had the limits defined again for him: You can go to a rock concert with friends, but you cannot ride in a car driven by a known drinker.

7. Clarify a Position

Limits may be defined, but they also need to be clarified sometimes. It is an essential aspect of firmness and assertiveness as a parent that your position be clear, well stated, and repeated, if necessary.

Parents need to be direct and to the point in stating what

is or isn't allowed, especially when a young person argues or takes the situation further after limits have been defined. That's when clarifying a position may be crucial. An assertive, firm parent will not become angry, furious, or out of control. Instead, he will continue to repeat the position and clarify exactly what it is he expects or will not allow.

To a teenager who wants money drawn out of his bank account to buy cassette tapes when he has previously agreed with his parents to save the money for school clothes: "The agreement was to save the money. I will not draw it out for this reason." To a child who insists on an ice cream treat from the refrigerator just before lunch: "No ice cream. It is almost lunch. I will not let you have ice cream now."

8. Provide New Rules as Necessary

In addition to reminding kids of rules and defining limits, sometimes you need to provide new rules for them. When a new problem pops up, a new rule often has to be invented. While kids may complain, they usually understand when a good, rational reason is offered.

This does not mean that rules are always being changed nor does it mean that you are inconsistent or that the basic ground rules are shifting. It indicates that as children develop and as family circumstances change, new rules have to be created.

When your sixteen-year-old starts driving the family car, for instance, new rules are needed to handle the changed circumstance. It was not necessary to have rules about driving before, but now it is. These new rules should be clearly stated: rule 1, no drinking and driving; rule 2, no using the car if your homework isn't done; rule 3, don't bring the car home with less than a quarter tank of gas. Even the consequences for violations of these new rules might be stated: If you break one of the rules about driving, you will not be allowed to use the car for a week.

Sometimes new rules come about because a new problem is occurring. Jenny's teacher told her parents at a school conference that she frequently fell asleep in her sixth- and seventh-hour classes. In talking to her about it, her parents discovered that she was napping after school and staying up late to watch TV. They solved the problem with a new rule: "From now on, you are not to take a nap after school or watch TV after 10:00 P.M."

As adolescents go out more with friends and begin dating, new rules become necessary. Young people seem to understand that if they are not dating yet, having a rule about the age they can start dating or with whom they can go out is silly. But when they are in high school, it becomes a central issue in many teenagers' lives. Some new rules can be provided: "You must be sixteen before you can go out on a date in a car" or "I must meet the boy you plan to date before you go out."

9. Make Requests

Although it has not been stated as a discipline technique up to this point, making requests has been implied. Using requests can be a suitable alternative to making demands and giving orders—techniques that often invite trouble in dealing with children.

Requests should be distinguished from commands. With commands ("Do not leave the yard today"), there is no option. It is not a request, it is an order and compliance is expected. Requests, on the other hand, indicate an option.

Many parents confuse commands and requests in the belief that if they are polite and respectful ("Would you mind doing the dishes?"), their child will be compliant. However, in making the request, the parent does not want to hear "No." When the child doesn't comply with what the parent saw as a reasonable request, the parent must now reveal the request as the command that it was.

If there is no option, make it easier on everyone and give a command.

Making requests, though, feels better for many parents. It implies respect and shows politeness and courtesy. Often children and teenagers respond much better to requests than they do to orders.

"Do you mind washing the dishes tonight?"

"Would you take time out from your video game and help me fold your clothes?"

"When you come home from the basketball game tonight, would you please take care of your chores?"

These are appropriate requests. But what if your child does not agree or just says no?

If it is a real request, you can accept that your child did not wish to do what you requested. If it is important to you that your child does something he agreed to do, you have some options. One option is to state: "I asked you politely to finish your chores and you haven't done so. Now I'm not asking. You must do them by tomorrow morning." Another way of handling it is to use an appeal, a discipline discussed in the next chapter, or to use a warning ("If you don't finish your chores by tomorrow morning, you won't be able to go out until they are finished"), a discipline skill discussed in more detail in chapter 11.

10. Hold a Gripe Session

Another way to prevent greater problems is to hold a gripe session. Children, like adults, need a chance to get things off their chest from time to time. As parents, we sometimes get

too busy and forget about giving our kids opportunities to ai
their grievances. Building into the family routine a good, old-
fashioned, let-your-hair-down gripe session periodically can go
a long way toward easing tensions in the family.

Mrs. Allen saw her three kids getting sore with each other
often. It looked as if a fight could break out at any moment if
something wasn't done to head it off. Instead of yelling, threatening, or lecturing, Mrs. Allen tried bringing all three kids
together and giving each a chance to spout off. What she heard
usually started with "I'm sick and tired of . . ." or "I don't know
why you don't do something . . ."

Mrs. Allen listened as each of her children expressed their
complaints. The opportunity to voice their feelings and anger
let her children get important resentments off their chests. At
the same time, Mrs. Allen learned that she was sometimes
contributing to tensions in the family when she handled problems in ways her children considered to be unfair. Together
they were able to devise new ways to solve some of the problems they'd uncovered.

When fourteen-year-old Krista snapped at her mother for
the third time in three days ("What do you care!"), her mother
knew there was a lot of anger brewing and it was time to have
a gripe session. Waiting until Krista cooled off, her mother
began, "Tell me what's bothering you lately." She wasn't sure
that she was going to be able to handle what she started when
Krista responded, "You!"

But it got better as her mother did more listening and less
talking and allowed Krista to be angry and even disrespectful
at first. Within a few minutes, Krista was crying and talking
about a teacher criticizing her, her boyfriend lying to her, and
her mother putting down the same boyfriend.

While she recognized that she wasn't always open-minded
about Krista's boyfriends and she didn't usually let Krista express anger toward her, her mother used this gripe session to

dump a lot of bad feelings she'd been carrying
process, their typical, unpleasant clash was
mother admitted some of her own gripes as
her own faults to Krista.

oth resolved to do better; Krista apologized for
snapping at her mother so much, and some emotional fences
were mended between them.

Call them gripe sessions, family meetings, or just talks, the
idea is the same. Set aside time regularly—once a month or
more often if needed—for the family to share feelings or
thoughts about problems or issues of importance.

Parents should take responsibility for initiating such sessions, but they should not dominate the meeting or use them
to pontificate or preach. Instead, parents can get the meetings
going and encourage open discussion of feelings, complaints,
and problems. They may also serve to put limits on behavior
and help to guide discussion when feelings run too strong and
threaten to spill over into verbal or physical attacks.

They should see to it that all family members have a chance
to speak and that no one is intimidated or ridiculed for expressing what he thinks or feels.

To end such meetings, there usually needs to be some
common agreement about problems and how they will be
resolved. This could very well lead to future meetings (set at
a specific date and time) to review decisions, monitor solutions,
and discuss additional or new problems or tensions.

11. Isolate the Child

In chapter 11, I will discuss using time-out as a punishment.
Isolation is different and can be a useful discipline technique
at times.

Isolating children means removing them from a situation
in order for them to gain control over themselves.

This is not punishment. Children are not necessarily doing anything bad when isolation is called for. They may be irritating, obnoxious, or silly. Or they may be overly stimulated and need an opportunity to get themselves under better control. One way to do this is to remove them, by your request, from a situation.

If eight-year-old Carlos is acting very silly at the dinner table, ask him to leave and go to his bedroom until he is under control. This can be done by making a simple request or command: "Carlos, why don't you go to your room until you're over your silly streak."

In public places, children often get "out of control." If two children begin to giggle in church, one or both of them may need to be isolated so that the giddiness of the moment can be brought under control.

Many situations can best be handled by removing the child. This works best if you have a good relationship with your child and are not angry, hostile, or out of control yourself when you isolate the youngster. Often a firm request ("Go to your room until you've calmed down") will be all that's needed. If it's not, try other options in this and later chapters.

IT MAY BE TRITE to remind you that an ounce of prevention is worth a pound of cure. But in parenting, this maxim carries considerable weight. Why allow your child to have a problem if you can prevent one from developing by applying your attention and love? The discipline techniques offered in this chapter can help you to be a preventive parent rather than a reactive parent. Your children might not thank you, but you'll feel considerable gratification when the family's problems and conflicts diminish.

Summary

The following discipline techniques can help to prevent problems in young people ages four to eighteen.

- Offer choices.
- Give rule reminders.
- Establish routines.
- Remove seductive objects.
- Plan in advance.
- Define limits.
- Clarify a position.
- Provide new rules as necessary.
- Make requests.
- Hold a gripe session.
- Isolate the child.

SEVEN

Techniques That Foster Self-control

THE ULTIMATE GOAL of all discipline is to teach children self-control. That's what parental discipline and child guidance is all about: Allowing our kids to grow up to be adults who can discipline themselves.

The techniques in this chapter have this goal particularly in mind. When we use these discipline techniques, we first of all give kids a chance to test their own self-control. Second, we monitor how well we are doing as parents by seeing how well our children are learning to control their own behavior and live with rules.

Suppose, for example, that Mr. and Mrs. Rosen have a sixteen-year-old daughter who is about to get her driver's license. One of Chris's problems relates to her anger and how she expresses it. When mad, Chris often slams doors and says outrageous, cutting, and sarcastic things to her parents and others. This indicates to Mr. and Mrs. Rosen that Chris has not learned to deal effectively with her anger.

Their greatest concern is that she might get angry while driving and do something reckless to endanger the car, herself, or others riding with her. One of their goals as parents is to help her discharge her anger more quickly and use better self-control. So the next time she gets angry at home, they can ignore her outburst and silently observe how long it takes her to bring herself under control. This way they can gauge how much progress she has made, how their discipline techniques are working, and whether she is ready to use the family car.

The techniques described in this chapter have some characteristics in common: They are all designed to encourage children to make greater use of their own self-control skills; they should be used before a child is out of control and before the misbehavior or problem behavior becomes too serious; they should generally be used while your youngster still has a chance of controlling the situation on her own.

When using these discipline skills, take into consideration how your child feels about you. If you have a fairly close and affectionate relationship with your child, these discipline techniques have a much greater chance of being effective. But if your relationship is characterized by conflict, hostility, resentment, or rebellion, these techniques can become provocation for further misbehavior or rebellion.

1. Ignore Behavior

The first such technique is ignoring. This is a very difficult skill for many parents to learn—or even accept. Many argue that ignoring a child is no technique at all. They feel that it is so simple and passive it amounts to doing nothing. Many parents assume they need to *do* something whenever kids misbehave. On the contrary, parenting experts recognize the power and usefulness of this technique—and the judgment required of parents to apply it effectively.

Ignoring children is not a passive way of avoiding your duty as a parent. Rather, it is the most benign and the mildest discipline skill you will ever use. It should not be used because you don't know what else to do. Instead, use it in a purposeful, planned way to assist children to curb their behavior or deal with problems on their own. It should be the discipline technique of choice when you are trying not to draw attention to a particular misbehavior.

By definition, ignoring is a technique in which you deliberately withhold attention from a child. It is best used for minor, irritating, or annoying behavior—especially when that behavior is intended to get your attention. Ignoring is to be used, then, whenever a bothersome behavior occurs.

As an example of effective ignoring, suppose you have a three-year-old who swears for the first time as you are watching television. Instead of drawing attention to the swear word and unintentionally reinforcing it by making mention of it, you can just ignore it.

Here's another example of the effective use of ignoring as a technique. Mr. Jensen noticed his two children having an argument on the back porch. He was near an open window and could overhear the progress of the squabble. Normally, he would break up their fights, but this time he decided just to listen and see how the children handled it.

"You're a liar," Timmy yelled at his sister.

"I am not," she countered. "You're a mommy's boy!"

The accusations went back and forth. Mr. Jensen restrained himself. Pretty soon, the tempers cooled off and both Timmy and his sister decided to play a game.

Mr. Jensen was amazed that when he stayed out of the argument, his kids were able to work it out and go on to play a game. Usually when he intervened, they stayed mad at each other for an hour or so and he ended up punishing both of them. He had learned a valuable lesson: If he ignored his children's conflicts, the kids could often settle them by themselves.

Some parents brought their son to see me because they were worried about his misbehavior, particularly his incessant name calling. Ralph called his parents and almost anyone else he met names such as shit-head and butt-wipe. He did this dozens of times a day, often at the most inappropriate and, for his parents, inopportune times. Their approach had been to scold him and punish him—all without any beneficial effect.

I taught Ralph's parents how to ignore him selectively. Since Ralph called me these and worse nicknames, I could sympathize; but I also demonstrated to the parents how and why ignoring Ralph's misbehavior was the discipline of choice. Ralph continued to call names, but the frequency declined—the fun was gone when he no longer got a rise out of me or his parents.

Two months later, Ralph's control over name calling, a misbehavior that had gone on over several years, had dramatically improved. From dozens of times a day, his name calling had dropped to an occasional "you're a jerk." When he did slip, his parents still ignored it—and Ralph sometimes even apologized. His father, who'd initially doubted that ignoring would work, now enthusiastically endorsed the technique.

Ignoring is an appropriate discipline technique to deal with such minor and annoying misbehaviors as whining, tattling, name calling, bedtime crying, sibling rivalry, swearing, and temper tantrums. These behaviors are often related to getting a parent's or another adult's attention.

There are times when ignoring is not appropriate. Anytime a behavior is dangerous or serious or could result in more misbehavior or peril for a child, ignoring would not be the technique of choice. Nor would it be in the child's best interest to ignore a youngster who is testing the limits to see what she can get away with—for instance, coming home late, failing to come in when called, hitting a parent, taking a car without permission, or stealing.

It would also be inappropriate to ignore a child who is already out of control and needs help. A child who is in the middle of a tantrum and about to do something harmful (throwing a glass or grabbing a knife, for example) needs to be restrained. However, this doesn't mean that ignoring shouldn't be used with temper tantrums. In fact, it is perhaps the most effective way to end a tantrum, as long as there is no violence involved.

When parents stay out of situations, they are showing that they have confidence in their children's ability to get themselves under control. It gives children a chance to work out their own problems and practice self-control. It is also a useful way to discourage inappropriate behavior: by not providing the attention, satisfaction, and negative reaction they are given for some misbehavior.

It is important to keep in mind that it is not your responsibility as a parent to solve all your children's problems or make sure that all difficulties are resolved in mature ways. Children have the right to try out coping skills on their own. Perhaps more important, they need to have the experience of dealing with difficult problems without parents intervening too quickly.

2. Give a Signal

A related but slightly more active technique, one that allows children an opportunity to pull themselves back together, is giving a signal. With this technique, you do not ignore the child, but you let her know that you are aware of the situation and that you expect her to gain self-control on her own.

Most parents have used this technique at one time or another; it often works well. At a movie or at a concert, I have nudged my children with an elbow when they were rustling their playbill or candy wrappers too loudly. That told them that I was aware of the noise they were making, that it was likely to be offensive to others, and that I expected them to stop the noise.

If a child is giggling with another child or whispering too loudly in church, a parent may tap the offending child on the shoulder or signal time out by making a T with two flat hands. This lets the child know that the parent is aware of the child's behavior. The parent delivers this message in hopes that this is the only one needed and that the child will take the necessary action to change her behavior so no further parental action is required.

Giving a signal alerts a child or teenager to a problem behavior. If that behavior occurs repeatedly, it is useful to develop a prearranged signal for the situation. Suppose, for instance, Elizabeth has a problem maintaining self-control in stimulating situations. When a large group of relatives are gathered together and lots of different activities are going on, Elizabeth is likely to get loud, obnoxious, pushy, and demanding.

Having recognized this as a problem, her parents can develop a signal for just such occasions. For instance, when she is at the point of losing control and becoming irritating and obnoxious, her father can give the agreed upon signal—say, cupping his hands as if he is holding a grapefruit. What this means to Elizabeth is that she is to recognize that she is losing control and needs to pull herself together.

Other signals may be clearing the throat, raising an eyebrow, making a slashing gesture with the hand across the throat, or just pronouncing the child's name.

This technique, like ignoring, can be used with children of all ages. It should be used when a misbehavior is about to begin or has just begun.

Giving a signal will be ineffective if the child is so manic from excitement or anger that she can't even recognize your presence. A group of eight-year-olds playing at a swimming pool on a hot day will probably not be paying enough attention to an adult to be aware of signals. A ten-year-old boy in the middle of a screaming fight with his sister will not notice your "look" or hear you clearing your throat.

If you have a fairly good relationship with your child or if you are consistent in your follow-through in discipline, giving a signal has a good chance of working. If not, then the use of a signal may indicate only that your child's behavior is getting your attention and may actually serve to reinforce the misbehavior.

3. Lend Your Ego

Another technique that allows children a chance to gain self-control is one I call *lending your ego*. What this means is that you can let your child borrow your ego (the management and control part of the personality) to bolster her own.

Since children's egos are not well developed, they sometimes need extra help in a crisis. That's where the parent can be helpful. Instead of expecting your child always to be in control, you may be prepared to step in to offer assistance when it appears your child will not be able to cope.

One way of lending your ego to a child is illustrated in the following story. Mrs. Hill glanced out her window one sunny day and saw her eight-year-old son Terry embroiled in an argument with a friend. She knew from past experience that when Terry reached a certain boiling point, he hit others. She watched for only a few seconds before she realized that Terry was quickly approaching his boiling point.

She went outside, walked up to Terry, and put her arm on his shoulder without saying anything. As soon as Terry felt his mother next to him, he turned and said, "Billy doesn't play fair!" Before Mrs. Hill could say anything, Terry said, "I'm going to play by myself in the house." He went into the house and a fight was avoided.

Parents can lend their ego strength to children by letting them know they are willing to help during a crisis. They can do this by making a remark or asking a question: "Anything I can do to help?" or "Let's see if we can straighten out this situation." They can also do it silently by just standing close to a child or, as Mrs. Hill did, by placing a hand on the child's shoulder.

Lending ego strength is especially helpful when children are anxious. Consider how often children are fearful of a new or difficult situation (adults too, for that matter). Children may be frightened of doing something by themselves, going to a new school on the first day, going to the doctor's office, or talking to a teacher about a problem in class.

If you offer to accompany your child, you can join forces with her so that she borrows some of your strength and support to handle the problem. She's still done it on her own, but you were behind her giving support.

It is common for children to be afraid of situations they have never faced before. When six-year-old Cliff was brought to my office for what his mother saw as a developing school problem, he grew increasingly apprehensive in the waiting room. When it was Cliff's turn to come into the office to speak with me, he shrank back in his chair, asked his mother if she were ready to go home, and refused to accompany me. "No way!" was he going anywhere with anybody, he said.

Cliff's mother quickly sized up the situation and knew that neither threats nor promises would work with her son. I suggested that she come with him. She held out her hand and in a calm voice said, "I'll go to the office with you and stay as long as you like."

Hesitantly, Cliff reached for her hand and began walking slowly to my office. Once there, she sat in a chair and we both allowed Cliff to explore the office. I pointed out some of the toys and books, and Cliff began to focus less on the frightening aspects of the situation and more on the interesting playthings available. I motioned to his mother to make an exit. She got up and said, "I'll be in the office across the hall. Call me when you need me."

Cliff barely looked up as she left, although he certainly heard her. A few minutes later, he wandered over to the door and peered anxiously across the hall. He was relieved to see her sitting there reading a magazine. Reassured, he returned to my office and continued a game he was by now playing with me.

A week later, when Cliff returned for his second visit, Mom's ego wasn't needed. Cliff acted like a veteran as he eagerly accompanied me to my office.

While effective in bolstering a child with a weak ego, this technique needs to be used with care. It must be suited to the likes and dislikes of a youngster and should not be forced on a child. Offering to lend your support ("Would it be helpful if I went with you when you talked to your teacher?") is one thing; taking over ("We're going up to the school and give your teacher a piece of our mind") is quite another. A young person, particularly a preadolescent or adolescent, may be embarrassed and feel demeaned if you take over a situation, especially in front of others.

Some children don't like to be touched. Others, if angry or out of control, may misinterpret a touch or an attempt to lend support as interference or physical restraint. Lending an ego must be suited to the personality of the child.

4. Hold a Child Firmly

A discipline technique that goes beyond the support of lending your ego is holding a child firmly. This is a physical technique, but should not be confused with spanking or corporal punishment, which will be discussed in a later chapter.

Holding firmly is a way of giving children support to stop them from continuing behavior they cannot stop themselves. This is most useful with younger children, especially those who are two, three, or four years of age.

Holding firmly involves physically restraining a child with a gentle but firm grip. It is useful with children who are out of control, unable to respond to directions, or unable or unwilling to stop a misbehavior. It is often necessary to hold a child to let the youngster know that you are firm, that you expect behavior to be controlled, and that you are willing to back up your commands.

Consider the case of three-year-old Jeffrey. He is a bright, highly verbal boy, but because of physical abuse from his father and frequent absence by his mother, he is angry and disobedient. When his adult baby-sitter or his mother tries to check his misbehavior, he sometimes loses control, throwing his shoes into the toilet, running through the house screaming, or kicking and biting. Because he has such poor control over his own impulses, restraint and holding are called for.

With Jeffrey, it is necessary to hold him firmly but without roughness when he can't stop himself. It is also necessary to talk him down at the same time. When Jeffrey is most out of control and angry, his mother holds him and says in her calmest, most controlled and soothing voice, "All right, I've got you. . . . Easy. . . . I'm not going to let you hurt yourself or anyone else. Calm down, relax. You're safe with me now." As she repeats this, he gradually stops squirming and relaxes. Then the outburst is over.

Young children who have not yet mastered their impulses may act wild and seem unable to put limits on themselves or refrain from breaking house rules. Holding lets them know that you are able to offer them protection (from their impulses) and that you will use firmness (but not harshness). When three-and-a-half-year-old Colleen throws toys and her father's books around and does not respond to "Stop!" or "Don't throw toys," holding her helps her to learn to stop herself.

There are some dangers and risks with this technique for the parent. One is that a very angry child may kick, bite, or scream. In holding or physically restraining a youngster, be sure you do it in such a way that she cannot hurt you (or that you do not hurt her). It can take a lot of strength.

A big, long bear hug, in which you wrap yourself around a child, can be effective even with angry children. Add lots of soothing talk and many children who start out attempting to strike out at the parent will be able to become calm.

It can be unsettling to some parents when children who are being held complain that you are hurting them or cry. This sometimes leads to halfhearted attempts to use this technique. In the long run, if you use this technique in an unsure way, you may be teaching your child that you cannot be firm and that you cannot protect her from herself.

Some children do not like restraint and others simply do not like to be held, cuddled, or touched. While this technique is not to be viewed as punishment, it may feel like a punishment to some youngsters. It is appropriate to remind you at this point that not every technique in this book will be effective with every child. This is one that should only be considered for use with young children who are out of control and cannot stop their own behavior.

5. Use Humor

Another way parents can support a child's self-control is by using humor. This can be a very effective way of calling attention to a problem while letting the child solve it. By making a joke, you are telling the child that you know there is a problem, but you're not going to take any action—at least not yet. You are also saying you don't regard the problem as serious and you have confidence the child will do something about it.

Children of all ages enjoy humor and a joke. Preschoolers begin to develop a sense of humor and can tell when a joke is intended if it is made obvious enough. One of the great advantages of humor with children is that they know you are not mad at them, although you are letting them know that something needs to be changed.

When Mr. McCarthy drove into his driveway as he returned home from work, he had to brake to a quick stop to avoid running over his daughter's ten-speed lying in front of the garage. His first reaction was anger—after all, he had told her a thousand times to keep her bike out of the driveway. And he had shouted in anger at her before. As he got out of the car and removed her bike, he began to cool down and decided to try a different approach. A couple of minutes later, he sauntered into the family room and said matter-of-factly, "Debbie, the most amazing thing happened today. I've heard of this gang of outlaws that goes around causing mischief by placing kids' bikes in the driveway so fathers run over them. They've struck in this neighborhood, and in fact, they did it to us!"

"I'm sorry, Dad," replied Debbie, holding back a grin. "I'll make sure that gang doesn't find my bike anymore."

Because of the joke, Debbie not only got the point but still liked her father. She wasn't angry; she was more amused and relieved that he scolded her in a palatable way. Mr. McCarthy felt better about this approach and gave himself a pat on the back for being so clever.

Children often expect an angry reprimand or a scolding or lecture. Surprising them by using humor may be one way of varying your scolding while also giving them an idea of what they have to change. If you do this before a problem has occurred or in the midst of a problem behavior, you alert the child that she has to use her resources to avert a misbehavior.

Here's a situation in which humor helped stem a developing problem: At the Hamptons' house there had been considerable conflict and tension about fifteen-year-old Pete's smoking. "We forbid you to smoke in the house or even on our property" was the decree from Mr. Hampton. He was supported by Mrs. Hampton, but Pete couldn't stop smoking and didn't really want to try anyway. When Pete was suspended from school for smoking and caught once again with cigarettes in his pocket, it appeared that another showdown was imminent. Pete and his father stared at each other as Mr. Hampton reached in his son's jacket pocket and pulled out the pack of cigarettes.

"Could I borrow a smoke, son?" asked Mr. Hampton. He could have sworn later in retelling this story that the tension literally drained out of Pete's face. Instead of an argument or shouting match, Pete gave up the cigarettes to his father and apologized for "forgetting" and bringing them into the house. "I'll try to remember to leave them somewhere else," Pete said, and then added, "I don't really mean to cause you and Mom trouble over this."

Pete needed a reminder that his controls weren't working as well as they should. A joke by his father eased the tension and allowed him to use his self-control to apologize and redouble his efforts to obey the rules.

Humor is best used when there is a fairly good relationship between parent and child. It should never become sarcastic.

Nor should a put-down be disguised as humor. Many parents use sarcasm and one-liners that remind children of their inadequacies without helping them do better at solving problems. Humor must avoid making kids feel small, inadequate, or incompetent. Humor and joking should also improve the relationship between parent and child. If it serves to cause hostility and decrease the rapport, then it is inappropriate or misguided. This will happen if the joke is made at the expense of the child.

For instance, if you say, "I suppose that candy bar walked into your pocket," after a child has been caught shoplifting, there is no humor here—it's sarcasm and undermines what the child feels toward herself and the adult.

However, in a similar situation, if you fake an Inspector Clouseau accent and say, "Ze master detective has discovered a clue!" the child may be slightly relieved and better able to answer the obvious question you're going to put to her.

It doesn't mean you don't appreciate the seriousness of the offense, but it lets the child know that you're not making a federal case out of it and that she's still welcome as a member of the human race.

Finally, humor *cannot* be used with children who are too sensitive and perceive put-downs when they are not intended. Some children, unfortunately, think others are laughing at them; when this is so, humor must be used very cautiously and judiciously.

6. Chart Problems

Charting is a way some parents have used to track the frequency of a problem. Here, however, it is not listed as a diagnostic tool for parents, but as a disciplinary technique to be used with children to give them a device to monitor themselves.

In using this technique, a parent talks to a child about a problem that has already been identified. The parent suggests that the child keep track of the time and frequency of a problem behavior. Other than helping a youngster develop a simple chart, that's all the mother or father does initially. After the child has had a week or two to monitor her own behavior, the parent can ask how it's going and check the progress.

Let's use an example. Joey was a six-year-old with a bladder-control problem. He frequently wet his pants when playing outside or walking home from his bus stop. His mother was worried that he would be rejected by other kids if he didn't try to get better control over the behavior.

She discussed the problem in this way and, without being critical, suggested that they try an experiment. She helped him make a chart. For two weeks he put ticks on his chart every time he wet his pants when outside.

What his mother had effectively done was to give him a way to draw his own attention to the extent of the problem and shift responsibility for the problem from herself to Joey.

The results for Joey? After a week of charting, he was more aware of the problem and began to come in more often to use the bathroom before he had an accident. By looking over his chart, his mother found that he had reduced the number of accidents from the first to the second week. It seemed obvious to her that Joey was actively working on the problem.

Charting can also be useful to help children with problems of fighting, hitting, tattling, leaving their seat at school, complaining about doing their chores, or failing to complete their school work. Parents and teachers who use charting with children and teenagers report that it helps both the adult and young person to better identify and define problems. For instance, in one family, the father complained about his daughter being disrespectful to him. When she agreed to chart this behavior, they had to decide exactly what *disrespectful* meant. For the first time, they had a discussion of this problem instead of an argument.

Other parents find that charting encourages kids to take responsibility for their own behavior and not depend on their parents stopping them through punishment or scolding. Many young people make an effort to improve their behavior when they see for themselves how often they are doing something both they and the adult would like to stop. It is better for most young people to make this discovery on their own through charting than hear angry parents tell them what they are doing wrong.

7. Provide Encouragement

Providing encouragement is a way parents can support their children's efforts to do well or to avoid trouble. Most children thrive on encouragement. It helps them to sustain their efforts performing tasks, doing school work, or maintaining good behavior.

Encouragement is best used when children are in danger of losing control or when they need some extra support, positive words, or a renewed feeling of hope. Children need encouragement after a less than successful effort at school or at a game, when they have suffered a defeat, or when they have had several discouraging things happen in a short space of time.

Children need encouragement from adults to know they are basically doing all right. Encouragement helps them to feel good about themselves, bolsters their self-control, and lends renewed energy to their efforts. If a child is about to lose control in an argument, the adult's role may be to remind her how well she's been doing lately and how she has been keeping her temper under control. Sometimes that is all that's needed for the control system to work.

When Kenny was working on a homework assignment at the dining room table, his father could see that he was struggling and becoming frustrated. His father feared that he might get angry, feel overwhelmed, or give up. Casually, his father walked by the table and looked over Kenny's shoulder.

"Hey, Kenny, you're doing well! You've got the first few problems right and I like the way you've taken your time and lined up the numbers in columns. If you keep this up, you're going to be done in a few minutes and it's going to be homework you'll be proud to hand in to Mr. Woodruff."

Kenny beamed, forgot about his frustration, and went back to work with increased confidence.

Encouragement, of course, calls for parents to use positive and supportive words. That means including reminders about how well a child is doing, how much progress or improvement they've noticed, and how close to finishing or completing a task the child seems to be.

There is no room for criticism or reminders of previous failure when giving encouragement—that would be contradictory and confusing. Encouragement should also be sincere, accurate (don't say she's been doing a good job if she hasn't!), and individualized to suit your child.

Encouragement doesn't always produce the expected effect; some children may give up or slack off when they receive encouragement. If that's true of your child, then be selective in its use. Be attuned to how your child responds to encouraging words, and then use those that are going to help her continue her efforts or gain better control.

8. Make an Appeal

A disciplinary technique designed to help children develop self-control is making an appeal. As the name implies, this technique involves appealing to a child: You directly request that the child pay attention to her behavior and to some other kind of standard—for instance, her view of herself as a fair or helpful person.

For example, fifth-grader Lenore had great difficulty getting along with other children. She frequently overreacted to playful teasing or taunts with hostility and rage, which made other children dislike her. Her mother was trying to help her with this problem. On her own, Lenore decided to make what she called an "oath": "I swear to treat other people kindly and not get angry when they tease me."

After making this vow to herself, Lenore came home from school one day and told her mother that she planned to get even with Amanda, who had teased her about being a "skinny minny." Her mother decided that an appeal was in order.

"You made an oath to treat others in a kind way, even when they are teasing you," began her mother. "Are you sure that by getting back at Amanda, you're acting like the kind person you want to be?"

Lenore had no choice but to admit that she wouldn't think of herself in that way if she got even. "I guess I'll think of something kind I can do instead," Lenore promised before bouncing off to get a snack.

By making a direct appeal, parents call attention to lapses in some standard or some value a child holds. They remind the child that she needs to use her self-control to come closer to that value or standard.

In another situation, Robert was picking on a smaller boy. His father didn't want to criticize him because he knew that Robert usually became surly or pouty when criticized. Instead, he decided to appeal to Robert's sense of fair play.

"Robert, when you pick on Timmy, I don't think you are being fair to him. You are bigger and stronger than Timmy. I know you want to be fair because I've heard you say that that's important to you." Robert got the message.

Appeals can be very effective with children who hold values and standards you know about. That suggests you need to understand your child well enough to be aware of what standards your child is striving to meet. This technique will obviously not work with a youngster who has an "I don't care" attitude or is too hostile or angry. Children who generally try to do well and attempt to please adults are the best candidates for this discipline skill.

9. Use Reasoning

Reasoning is a special kind of appeal. Obviously, many parents say they use reasoning when, in fact, they are attempting to use their authority or the force of their arguments to bring about compliance with their requests or commands.

As described in this section, reasoning is a way of conveying information to a child. By giving a youngster information she might not have had previously, the mother or father is allowing her to use her own reasoning ability without being forced to "obey" the parent's orders.

It is essential in order for children to develop their ability to think and solve problems, as well as to develop inner controls, that they learn to use information. The only way for this to happen is for parents to provide them with that kind of opportunity. Instead of telling a child "Do it because I said so" or "Do what I said because I'm the parent," explaining the reason behind the directive provides information and appeals to the child to use that information in a constructive way by making a mature decision.

Mr. Fielder was concerned because the rap music his eleven-year-old son was listening to on the car's tape cassette player was sexist and demeaning to women. As he listened to the music, he sorted through his potential responses. When the tape was finished, he elected to reason with his son by giving him information about the music.

"When you listen to that group again," Mr. Fielder began, "pay attention to the lyrics. If you listen very closely to the words that group sings on this tape, I think you'll hear some of the same things I heard. Their lyrics talk about women only as sexual objects. That's not what your mother and I believe is a healthy way of thinking about girls or women."

Mr. Fielder gave his son some information he may not have been aware of before. He was also reasonable and not argumentative. He did not demand his son stop listening to the music and he didn't punish him or threaten to take the tape away. He made precise statements based on facts and his own personal values. All of this was conveyed in a conversational way that was easy for the boy to understand.

Using the technique of reasoning requires that a parent use information to appeal to the child's rationality rather than use parental authority to overpower a child into obedience. The parent does not say "I know best" but "Here is some valuable information that you should know; it's up to you to make a decision given this information."

Charlotte, a teenager, made plans to stay overnight at her girlfriend's house with her mother's permission. Later in the evening, her mother received a phone call from the mother of Charlotte's friend. Both girls had sneaked out the window and were nowhere to be found. Charlotte's mother was very upset, and when there was still no word about Charlotte's whereabouts several hours later, her anxieties turned to panic.

She couldn't sleep. She took the car out and drove around hoping to find the girls. She finally gave up and went home to wait it out. Charlotte called the next morning and said she was on her way home to explain.

When she arrived home, her mother's impulse was to yell, reprimand, and maybe ground her for a long time. Holding back these impulses, she listened to her daughter's explanation.

"Mary was planning to run away and I wouldn't let her go, at least not alone. I was worried that she might get into trouble or get hurt on her own," Charlotte explained.

This was plausible to her mother; she knew Charlotte was a compassionate young person. Also, she knew Charlotte had no particular reason to run away herself.

She thought that it was best to give information to Charlotte so that the next time such a situation came up, Charlotte might choose a different course of action.

"I was frantic when Mary's mother called and said the two of you were gone. I couldn't imagine what happened to you. My fears turned to panic and I couldn't sleep all night.

"I believe what you did was well motivated, but there were ways that you, too, could have been hurt. Two teenage girls on the street late at night in this city is very dangerous. You are not a street-smart person although you are intelligent and kind-hearted.

"You could have avoided causing me and Mary's mother so much worry by calling, leaving a note in Mary's room, or just bringing her here."

Reasoning, as a discipline technique, is important at every age so children can learn to think for themselves and develop self-control. Not every child can make good use of this technique, but if it is begun at an early age and used frequently, children can become more skillful as they develop.

A parent should not rely on this discipline skill any more than any other one. There are times, of course, when a child is not prepared to reason or think in a logical manner (or listen to reason). It is not used appropriately when it turns to argument or a conflict develops between parent and child.

Summary

Parents can encourage children to use and develop self-control through the following discipline techniques:

- Ignore behavior.
- Give a signal.
- Lend your ego.
- Hold a child firmly.
- Use humor.
- Chart problems.
- Provide encouragement.
- Make an appeal.
- Use reasoning.

EIGHT

Techniques That Teach Lessons

THE GOAL of the discipline techniques described in this chapter is to help young people deal with problems in new or different ways. Insofar as they are nonpunitive, they are like the discipline skills aimed at preventing problems. But their particular focus is to teach children lessons and skills that will enable them to cope with problems in the present and avoid them in the future.

Teaching a lesson can mean different things to different people. There's a big difference between teaching to educate and illuminate and teaching to punish. Too often, parents who say they are teaching their kid a lesson end up using that as a rationalization for physical abuse. Over the years, I've worked with many parents who were charged with abusing their children. Never did any of these mothers or fathers say their goal was to hurt their children. Most said they intended to teach their youngsters a lesson. Indeed, every parent wants to teach children how to do right. But frequently the techniques parents choose fall far short of their lofty goals, and the lessons their children learn end up hurting their chances of adjusting well to life.

The techniques discussed in this chapter, if used appropriately and as described, will not hurt or punish children but will help them learn a moral lesson, or think about their actions and take steps to act differently.

That may not be your first thought at a time when hassles have piled up, the kids are acting sassy, and you've reached your wits' end; then, you're not likely to be concerned about whether children think about their behavior—you just want them to stop driving you nuts. Keep in mind, though, that guiding children to look inward and reflect on why certain problems take place enables them to figure out what they might do to change. It's worth the investment of your time and effort to foster this sort of self-reflection, for the long-term yield is greater self-awareness and self-discipline for your child. These techniques are designed to have a greater chance of bringing about genuine self-reflection than the old parental command to "Go to your room and think about what you've done!"

As our children grow up and become independent, it is only through learning to use problem-solving skills that they will be able to function away from us (or from other authority figures) and make difficult decisions on their own. We don't always want to be there to guide them and tell them what is right and what is wrong. Before they are on their own, making critical judgments for their own life, we have to prepare them. That's what this chapter is all about.

One further point. These approaches are calm, adult responses to problem behaviors and situations. When you use them, you must treat kids with respect and as young adults if they are to have a good chance of working. When they are used well, both you and your children can come away feeling good about the experience.

1. Ask Think Questions

The first technique is to ask think questions. This skill can be used with a child of any age, starting with the misbehaving toddler who has some beginning language skills.

Asking think questions means asking questions that force children to explore reasons for their behavior and actions. They require young people to be reflective and to use their thinking and reasoning abilities. Think questions can be used after a child has misbehaved or displayed poor judgment, before a parent imposes a punishment, and when you are attempting to better understand the reasons for inappropriate behavior.

Here's an example of the use of this technique.

Ms. Nelson told three-year-old Kellie several times to play away from the street in their subdivision and never to cross the street by herself. One spring afternoon, Mrs. Nelson looked up from her kitchen work to notice that Kellie was no longer playing in the backyard. She began searching for her and discovered her at a neighbor's yard five doors down and across the street. Instead of yelling, reprimanding, or reminding her of the rule, Mrs. Nelson asked a question that forced Kellie to think about her action.

After telling Kellie she had to come home and go indoors, she took Kellie by the hand and walked her home. As they walked, Mrs. Nelson asked: "Kellie, do you know why I'm taking you home and why you have to stay in the house for the rest of the afternoon?"

Kellie responded immediately. "Yes," she said.

"Tell me why," her mother said.

" 'Cause I went to Billy's and wasn't supposed to."

"Why not?" Mrs. Nelson asked

" 'Cause I'm not supposed to cross the street," Kellie replied.

"That's right," Mrs. Nelson said firmly, but without anger. "Our rule is that you must not cross the street without asking me first."

By asking those think questions, Mrs. Nelson was accomplishing more than one thing. She discovered Kellie knew what the rule was. Kellie heard herself repeat the rule—a way for the rule to be reinforced in her mind. And Mrs. Nelson was teaching her daughter that when a rule was violated there would be a negative consequence. Asking a think question further emphasized that Kellie was not being punished because her mother was mad at her; it was because she had broken an important rule, one she knew about and could remember.

Mrs. Nelson could feel somewhat comforted by the fact her rules were lodged in Kellie's memory, even if her daughter didn't always follow them.

If Kellie had not remembered the rule, asking the think question would have made that plain as well. So if Kellie had said no instead of yes, Mrs. Nelson could have gone on to repeat the rule, realizing that it needed additional emphasis and that she might have to test Kellie again to make sure the message had gotten through.

The same technique can be used with older children, but altered to suit the child's age level and degree of maturity. If you have a fourteen-year-old who comes in late at night, you might use a think question in the following way:

"Todd, do you remember what time you said you'd be home?"

Now, Todd is going to answer either with a yes or no depending on how the question is asked. If it is asked in a sarcastic way, you might get a sarcastic answer in return. If asked in a calm, straightforward way, the answer usually—

although certainly not always—will be an equally straight response. Your next statement and question will be important.

If he doesn't remember what time he was to have been home, you will say something like this: "It bothers me that we make agreements and then you forget what they are when you leave home. This is not the first time this has happened and I'm wondering how we might handle this kind of thing differently so you don't forget. What do you think?"

If he does remember what the agreement was, your response is similar, but with emphasis on solving that basic problem: "Todd, it seems that you remembered what we agreed to and yet you still weren't home on time. What do you see as the reason that this sort of thing happens?"

With a fifteen-year-old who has run away, a think question is vital: "Bobbie, we were frantic with worry when we found out you left home. We don't want this to happen again, so what do you think we all have to do differently so you don't run away again?"

When the problems are more serious and the responses more critical, the answers don't have to be given immediately. Often teenagers need some time to think through a response, but a definite time should be arranged for further discussion so they don't get let off the hook by simply avoiding the issue.

When teenagers are evasive or respond with the traditional "I don't know" answer, a think question can be proposed that will be pursued at another time. You might say: "Running away is a serious way of dealing with problems and something must be wrong. Maybe you can't give me a good answer now, but think about it and let's talk again tomorrow evening after dinner. Will you try to come up with two things that you regard as serious problems here at home?"

Both children and teenagers often need "starters"—that is, options or alternatives that start them thinking. In talking to a young person about the reasons for some misbehavior (for instance, swearing at a teacher, which resulted in suspension), starters might be employed in the following way: "I know you said you don't know why this happened. However, I know that it has happened with other kids your age. Sometimes it happens to others because they were embarrassed by the teacher, or they were angry about something that happened at home before they went to school, or they had a problem with another student. Does any of this sound familiar? Could any of these reasons apply to you?"

You may not know the reason for the misbehavior, but often you can make a good guess. Asking a starter question will elicit some kind of response, even if you are incorrect in your guess. Kids will certainly let you know if the starter question is off the mark by correcting you. Then you can make an adjustment and ask a more appropriate question.

2. Tell Stories That Make a Point

Sometimes a different approach is called for when you're trying to get a child's attention and make a point. Telling stories that make a point can be very effective ways of teaching lessons.

All young people, and, of course, especially young children, enjoy a good story. If a story is interesting and entertaining, you can slip a moral or lesson into it and kids won't mind. While they may think they are just being entertained, you can be planting some important thoughts in their mind.

Consider twelve-year-old Sean, who had lived with his mother and her boyfriend for more than a year following his parents' divorce. Sean's mother wasn't able to provide much supervision for Sean, and his grades in school had declined. In addition, his behavior was frequently disorganized and he seemed unhappy about life.

His father, recently remarried, could see what was happening to Sean. He didn't want to fight his ex-wife for custody, yet he believed that his home life was more conducive to discipline and structure for Sean. He discussed the situation with Sean's mother, who agreed to let Sean live with him if the boy wanted to. So Sean was presented with a hard choice: Come to live full time with his father and stepmother or stay with his mother and continue to be unhappy.

Sean did not want to hurt his mother by telling her he didn't want to live with her anymore. He also didn't want to hurt his father by telling him there were things he liked about living with his mother. His father sensed Sean's confusion and told him a story:

"I know a boy who was about your age who had to make a decision just like the one you have to make.

"This boy's parents got a divorce and he had to decide which parent he would live with. Would he live with his mother, who provided discipline and supervision and was determined for him to finish school? Or with his father, who loved him but was more lax in his discipline and would let him do whatever he wanted to do?

"This boy chose his father. Later, he quit school and went into the army. Then he got married and had children. But, looking back on his life, he realized he had made a mistake; he made the wrong decision. He could have made so much more of his life if he had chosen differently at age twelve.

"Do you know who that boy was?"

Sean thought the story sounded familiar, but he didn't really know who the boy was.

"That boy was me," said his father. "Don't make the same mistakes I made."

Armed with support and a dramatic story from his father, who had packed a great deal of information into a fascinating true-to-life tale, Sean made the decision he knew in his heart was the right one to make. It was Sean's father's willingness to share something from his own life that provided Sean with the support he needed at a crucial time in his childhood.

Along with true stories, made-up stories can be used to get a point or lesson across. Most young children love stories in which there are animals or other children. If a six-year-old shows sadness related to the parents' divorce, one of the parents might tell a story like the one that follows. Such stories are often most successful at bedtime when youngsters are more relaxed.

"Once upon a time, there was a little boy—let's call him Teddy—who lived in a big white house with his mother. The reason he lived with his mother was that his parents were divorced. And do you know how Teddy felt about his parents' getting a divorce?

"He felt very sad, and sometimes angry, too. At times he was so sad, he didn't want to play or even eat his favorite food. Because of this, his parents were very worried about Teddy.

"Teddy was worried about himself, too. He felt so sad he didn't know if he would ever feel good again. So what do you suppose Teddy did to begin feeling better? [Asking questions and waiting for the child's response lets you know if the child is listening and how involved in the story he is.]

"No, that's not what Teddy did. He did not go on being sad and angry. What Teddy did was to ask a grown-up for help. And do you know who he asked for help?

"That's right. He went to his favorite adult, his Uncle Larry. One day Uncle Larry was visiting. Teddy asked if he could talk to him. He told Uncle Larry about how sad he felt. He said he felt sad and angry, too, because his parents got a divorce and they live in different houses. Then he asked Uncle Larry a very important question. Do you know what he asked him?

"No, he didn't ask if his parents would ever get married again. What Teddy did ask was this: 'What can I do to stop feeling sad when I think about my parents?'

"And his Uncle Larry had a very good answer. He told Teddy that children usually feel sad when their parents get a divorce and live in separate houses. They feel sad because they believe that their parents got a divorce because of the child. And sometimes they believe that their mother will leave them just as their father did.

"But children don't cause their parents to get a divorce. Divorces happen because of adult problems. Another thing is that parents don't stop loving their children when they get a divorce. Both Mommy and Daddy keep loving them just as much as when they lived together. And their mother never leaves them."

3. Role Play

Role playing, in which the parent plays one role and the child another, is another way of actively engaging children or teens in a learning and problem-solving process. Because role playing requires the active participation of a young person, it can be a very effective way to teach children to put themselves in someone else's place and to develop insight into their own thinking, feeling, and behavior. Role playing also allows kids to rehearse how they will handle problems and teaches them how to anticipate and prepare for situations.

Mrs. Pender used role playing with her daughter Mary in an effort to get a message across.

Mary was eight years old and a third-grader. A pretty child, she often seemed depressed, especially when she was overly critical of herself. This usually happened with her gymnastic endeavors, during a dance lesson, or when she was doing her homework for school. This bout of depression worried both Mrs. Pender and Mary's teacher.

Mrs. Pender wasn't quite sure how to handle it. Her impulse was to tell Mary to relax and not be so hard on herself.

But she had tried this before with no appreciable success. Out of desperation and a creative spirit, Mrs. Pender hit on the idea of using role playing.

"Mary, let's try something," Mrs. Pender said to her daughter one day after Mary returned from a dance lesson with another down-in-the-dumps look on her face. "I'm going to be you, Mary, and you're going to be a new girl at school. Your name is Sally, okay?"

Mary, who had been feeling blue, began to brighten up. She readily agreed to play along. Her mother started the role-play.

"Hi, Sally, I'm Mary. I'm glad you came to our school."

"Hi, Mary," said Sally. "It's nice to make a new friend on the first day of school."

"I'll bet you were scared coming to a new school."

"I sure was," said Mary in the role of Sally.

The conversation went on and a few weeks of developing friendship were compressed in a few minutes of fantasy play.

"Sally," began her mother, asking a question, "will you tell me something?"

"Sure," replied her daughter, not certain what was coming but involved in her role.

"Sally, tell me what you like about me."

Mary thought for a few seconds and said, "Mary, I like you because you work hard at school."

"Now, Sally, tell me what you don't like about me."

This time the answer came back quicker, but it was accompanied by an angry expression that surprised her mother. "Mary, I don't like it that you're so hard on yourself. It's not necessary to be mad at yourself when you don't always do well."

"Thanks for your honesty," said her mother, still in the role of Mary. "Sally, would you still like me if I wasn't always the best at everything?"

"Yes," said Mary, the anger of a few seconds ago now gone.

"You are a nice person no matter what you do on your report card or at dance class."

The role-playing game ended a few minutes later. Both Mrs. Pender and her daughter were happy with their play time together. No previous interchange between them had ever brought them this close. And Mrs. Pender was sure Mary had gotten more out of this than any lecture or discussion could have brought about.

Mary learned she already knew she was too hard on herself. It also reinforced some positive things about herself that she sometimes forgot or overlooked in her drive to be the best. It was not only a fun way to deal with an important problem, but Mary needed to take herself less seriously. Role playing was a step toward accomplishing this.

Role playing could be used to teach a child how to talk to a teacher about a grade the child thought was unfair. In this instance, the parent could begin by saying, "I know it's difficult to talk to your teacher, but let's try it here. First, I will be you and you be Mr. Henderson. I'll start by saying, 'Mr. Henderson, could I talk to you about that mark you gave me on my social studies report?'

"Now, you are Mr. Henderson. What would you say?"

Teenagers frequently become depressed and berate themselves when they cannot accomplish some task they believe they should master. One such task, especially for boys, is asking a girl for a date. Role playing this with a fifteen- or sixteen-year-old can provide an invaluable rehearsal for actually asking a girl out.

You could start by saying, "Look, let's play act this. To begin, I'll be you and I'll call a girl on the phone. You be the girl. Okay, here we go . . . I'm dialing and the phone is ringing. . . . You pick it up and what do you say?"

I've played such scenes with dozens of teens and heard how dating situations bring out their worst fears. (The main fear, of course, is rejection.) In role playing the young person has a chance to verbalize this: "She'll think I'm a total nerd" or "She'll laugh at me if I ask her to go out with me." With a parent directing this mini-play, the young person can confront and act out those "worst fears" in a less threatening situation. By role playing what would happen if a girl turned them down, for instance, they discover they can cope even with this ultimate rejection.

Stories can also be a way of teaching young people about family values and social responsibility in such areas as lying, stealing, tattling, and dealing with peer problems. Children often tune us out during lectures. Stories tend to engage children actively in the listening and understanding process. By stopping in the midst of stories and asking questions ("And do you know what the puppy's father did next when the puppy told the lie?"), you get immediate feedback about whether they are listening ("I think his father gave him a spanking"), or tuning you out ("No . . . I don't know").

There are some important points to keep in mind about telling stories. Like most other discipline and guidance techniques, it should not be overused or it will lose its effectiveness. If children have heard the same story about your childhood several times, they will stop listening. On the other hand, sometimes the same story or a slight variation will have to be repeated as many as three or four times for the child to begin to assimilate it and use it. Made-up stories are easier for children to accept as fiction and are less likely to be regarded as another form of a lecture.

These techniques cannot be relied on to solve all problems. Moreover, some children will respond better than others to stories. You have to know your child and what he likes in order to choose the most appropriate method of discipline.

4. Make an Interpretation

Making an interpretation means giving young people information that allows them to be more aware of their own feelings or behavior. This can be used with preschoolers occasionally, but is best reserved for children beginning at the early grade-school ages (ages six through eight), whose abstract thinking skills are more highly developed than they are at an earlier age.

In a sense, this is a cognitive restructuring technique. Children's thinking is slightly restructured because of the new insight provided by the adult: It allows them to view themselves in a new way, and then to integrate this insight into their thinking about themselves. If the youngster better understands the motives and reasons for his behavior, then he can make an adjustment of his own to change his behavior.

Here are examples of the use of this technique.

The Bergman family is making the three-hour drive to Grandmother's house for Thanksgiving dinner. Into the second hour, the two Bergman children—David, six, and Eric, nine—are excited but also bored and hungry. They start scrapping in the backseat, irritating Mr. Bergman, who is driving. Mrs. Bergman takes all of this in and makes a simple interpretative statement:

"I think you kids are getting tired and cranky because of the long drive to Grandma's. I'll bet you can hardly wait to get there, right? I think you're starting to fight with each other just because you're tired of riding so long. But we're going to be there in less than an hour."

Although that's all she said, it seemed to have a magical effect on the boys. They settled back in their seats and started to notice landmarks that proved they were indeed getting closer to Grandmother's house.

Eleven-year-old Eddie becomes angry and withdrawn whenever he is reprimanded or scolded. Sometimes the pouting and silent anger continues for more than a day when either of his parents has pointed out some flaw in his behavior. His parents wonder if he really is aware of how he acts and whether he sees his reaction as clearly as everyone else in the family sees it. They decide that pointing it out to him (making an interpretation) might help him respond differently.

"Eddie, you know how you've been angry and out of sorts during the last few days?" his father began. "Do you know why?"

"Naw, I've just been tired," said Eddie.

"You know what?" said his father. "I don't really think that's it. You know what I think?"

"What?" inquired Eddie.

"I've noticed something about you. Every time your mom or I scold you or tell you something we think you could improve, you get mad inside and then you go to your room or just shut us out. For days after that you mope around and feel mad and don't talk to us. Were you aware of that?"

"Well, sort of," ventured Eddie, not sure where this was going.

"Well, let me tell you," his father said, trying to keep this discussion light, "you act like we all have a dreaded disease. I'm not mad at you now and I'm not being critical. I thought it would help you to know what I see you doing. Okay?"

"Okay," said Eddie.

This may not end Eddie's typical reaction to scolding, but it gives him more information and insight into his own behavior. With this information he can choose to make a change. If it's not working well, at least his father has opened the door for more discussion about Eddie's withdrawal and silent anger.

The mother of twelve-year-old Maureen used interpretation a few months after the mother began a new dating relationship. The divorce had taken place more than two years before, and Maureen's father maintained regular visits with

Maureen, picking her up on weekends and attending as many of her soccer games as he could.

Maureen was understandably cool to Jerry, the first man her mother had dated seriously. As her mother and Jerry became closer and Jerry spent more time at her house, Maureen's behavior and attitude reflected her growing hostility.

Following two separate times in which Maureen was disrespectful and impolite to Jerry, her mother waited until her own anger had subsided and until she and Maureen were alone.

"I have been noticing how you act toward Jerry and I thought it was time for us to talk about it," her mother said. "You may not know why you act so rude to Jerry," she continued, "but I think I know."

"I don't like him," volunteered Maureen.

Her mother replied, "I think it's more than that."

Maureen was silent.

"I think that you actually think he's okay," said her mother. "But what you're having difficulty with is accepting a man— any man—that I like and who might replace your father. You're afraid of liking Jerry too much or getting too close to him because you might make your father jealous. You don't want to be disloyal to your father."

Maureen didn't respond, but she was listening intently. Her mother made a final comment: "Girls can love their father and also like the man their mother dates or even marries."

By making these kinds of interpretative remarks, parents help young people see the reasons for their feelings and behavior. It's important not to allow the interpretation to be an accusation or criticism but rather a neutral suggestion.

Suppose your teenage daughter constantly borrows her sister's clothes without permission and uses the excuse that "She borrows mine without asking." You realize that she is actually angry because her sister always outshines her at school. Pointing this out in a way that is neither critical nor condemning may help her view her own actions for what they really are.

Highly defensive or hostile young people are not good candidates for the use of this discipline technique because they will reject your interpretation. Those children and teenagers who are more open and less defensive will be more willing to accept new information in the form of interpretation.

5. Hold a Post-Event Discussion

When misbehavior is serious or significant, emotions and feelings—both child's and parent's—become strained. In the heat of the moment is not the best time to try to talk about what happened and why. Still, it has to be talked about. That's why a discussion after the event should be planned or even scheduled for a specific later time.

Parents I work with whose children are caught breaking and entering or dealing drugs or who run away or get suspended from school tell me they feel murderous rage and hysterical anger when they find out what their child has done. If the police call you in the middle of the night and ask you to come to the police station to pick up your son, you know that getting into a discussion right then will only lead to anger, criticism, or fighting. An all-night discussion—or interrogation, as it often turns out to be—under these circumstances may bring about alienation, perhaps more rebellion, and almost certainly no new knowledge about why the incident occurred.

The next morning, after everyone has had a chance to get some sleep (if that's possible for a mother or father who's just bailed a kid out of the slammer at 3:00 A.M.) and allow their emotions to settle, is a better time to try to get a handle on what happened.

In general, it's better to spend some time talking to your spouse, a friend, your minister, a therapist, or a relative who can help you calm yourself and get your feelings under control. You will need some perspective on the situation and a plan or idea about how you are to approach this post-event discussion.

Here's how one mother handled it when a three-hundred-dollar telephone bill came in. Her daughter had made many long distance calls to a boyfriend without her parents' permission. She waited two hours and thought it through before approaching her fifteen-year-old daughter.

"Debby, I got the phone bill today and I was too angry to talk to you before. Now I think I have my feelings under control and we need to talk. Take a look at this bill and see if you don't agree with me that we've got a serious problem. I thought that if we talked about it we could figure out how best to handle it."

In another family, nine-year-old Mark comes home from weekend visits with his father and stepmother with a definite chip on his shoulder. His mother and stepfather have noticed this after several visits. They believe that something has to be done. They have talked to each other and have agreed they will talk to Mark. However, they have purposefully waited until three days after the last visit to bring it up to him.

"Mark," says his mother, "we've noticed for the past couple of months that you act different when you come home from visits with your dad. You act more angry and unhappy with us. You snap at everyone and spend more time in your room alone. We're not sure why this happens and we need your help in understanding it."

This is a beginning. It is the beginnings that give most parents problems in post-event discussions. They often would like to rush in, ask why questions ("Why did you steal the money from you dad's dresser?") and risk a hostile and adversarial relationship.

In starting post-event discussions, the opening words are critical. Angry parents frequently make the tactical error of beginning with overdramatic accusations ("You must be on drugs. Is that why you broke into the house?") or attacking the young person directly ("How could you do something so incredibly stupid?").

Criticism, blaming, or threatening usually leads nowhere. It is generally better to start with an understanding comment showing concern for the child and his situation. Here are some sample openings for post-event discussion that have a chance of engaging a young person in the process.

- "You must be exhausted after what you've been through. Let's see if we can make some sense of all of this."
- "You must have been scared when the police officer put the handcuffs on you and threw you into the police car. What happened after that?"
- "There are so many things I don't understand about last night. Maybe you feel the same way. Let's go over things to see if I can understand things better."
- "Tell me about running away."

The opening of this kind of discussion must establish a rational, noncritical atmosphere in which the young person feels safe enough to talk about himself and his behavior. Zeroing in on feelings or motives by asking why questions ("Why would you break into cars?" or "Why did you steal the money? Don't we give you enough?") will surely block communication.

It is essential for parents to view a post-event discussion as a process that will not be concluded quickly and provide all the answers you want or need at one time or in one conversation.

To understand why serious misbehavior occurs takes patience, good listening skills, the ability to ask the right questions, and the restraint to keep yourself from resorting to preaching, moralizing, or losing control.

A post-event discussion should obviously end not only with more understanding of a behavior problem, but with some agreement as to how the problem or situation can be corrected or handled differently in the future.

Here is an example of a fruitful post-event discussion that took place after a fifteen-year-old was arrested for driving his mother's car while she was out of town. He was held in jail for several hours before his mother was summoned to pick him up and take him home. She was looking for answers the next day.

MOTHER: "Neil, we've got to talk."

NEIL: "Yeah, I know."

MOTHER: "I just couldn't believe it when the police called up. It wasn't right for them to hold you so long in jail. And handcuff you!"

NEIL: "It's not fair. I'm a minor."

MOTHER: "I know. But tell me what happened."

NEIL: "Well, I was driving your car and the police stopped me."

MOTHER: "Yes . . . and?"

NEIL: "That's all."

MOTHER: "Let's back up, okay?"

NEIL: "Okay."

MOTHER: "How did you get the keys to my car?"

NEIL: "You know. You always leave a spare set of keys in the drawer in the kitchen."

MOTHER: "Oh, yeah. I forgot about those. Okay. So you remembered the keys. But I'm not sure why you were going to use my car. You've never done that before."

NEIL: "Well, I wanted to help my friend."

MOTHER: "Bob?"

NEIL: "Yeah. His car wouldn't start and he needed a jump. He only lives down the street and I figured I would drive down there, give him a jump, and get the car back and no one would ever know. I thought if you did find out, you wouldn't mind. You like Bob."

MOTHER: "Yes I do. All right, so you took the keys to the car and drove down to Bob's and hooked on the booster cables?"

NEIL: "Right."

MOTHER: "Then what?"

NEIL: "Well, Bob got his car going and I was going back home, but Bob was afraid to use his car then and wanted a ride up to the mall. He was afraid his car would stall out again."

MOTHER: "You gave him a ride there?"

NEIL: "Yeah."

MOTHER: "Weren't you afraid of getting into an accident or getting stopped by the police—I mean, without having a driver's license?"

NEIL: "Yeah. I was thinking of that, but I had driven to Bob's and the mall wasn't that far. So I said I would."

MOTHER: "When did you get stopped by the police?"

NEIL: "That was after I saw some other guys at the mall. . . ."

MOTHER: "You parked and went into the mall?"

NEIL: "Well, just for a minute. . . . Bob and I stopped at the arcade and Al and Tom—you don't know them—were there. We talked and they needed a ride home."

MOTHER: "You took them home and then what?"

NEIL: "Al and Bob and I thought we would go over to this girl's house."

MOTHER: "What went on there?"

NEIL: "We talked with her and listened to music and that's all."

MOTHER: "There was some drinking?"

NEIL: "Not me! Al and Bob were drinking and I guess they brought some beer with them when I took them home."

MOTHER: "And that's when you were stopped by the police?"

NEIL: "I was almost home and this police car came out of

nowhere. . . . They asked to see my license and said I was speeding . . . I wasn't going that fast."

MOTHER: "They found beer in the car?"

NEIL: "Yeah. I said I wasn't drinking, but they said I was responsible and they put cuffs on me and threw me in the police car."

MOTHER: "I think there are some lessons to be learned from this, don't you?"

NEIL: "I guess so."

MOTHER: "What have you learned?"

NEIL: "Don't pick up guys who are drinking."

MOTHER: "I think there are some other lessons here. I'd like to go over these with you at another time. Also, when we have a chance tomorrow, I'd like to talk to you about your using my car and the issue of getting your license when you turn sixteen."

NEIL: "You mean I can't get my license when I'm sixteen?"

MOTHER: "I didn't say that. I just said we need to talk about it. Let's talk more tomorrow when I get home from the office."

NEIL: "Okay."

In this discussion, Neil's mother didn't get hysterical or uncontrollably angry. She didn't put Neil on the defensive and followed his lead by asking questions that brought out more information. Adolescents often leave out vital bits of information in telling about events, and a parent must pursue the information with relevant questions. The follow-up in this situation is indicated by the mother's suggesting a next time to talk and giving a brief agenda for the conversation.

By avoiding any accusations about Neil's "lying" to her and avoiding any suggestion that he too was drinking, she stuck to the facts as he was willing to tell them. She was in a position to make some educated guesses about Neil's thinking and his probable behavior. She can deal with his probable drinking, his level of responsibility, his poor judgment, and his need to please his friends at other times.

6. Teach Coping Strategies

Often children and teenagers don't have enough experience at solving problems and need to be taught coping strategies.

Young people are often forced to deal with situations they don't have the experience or knowledge to get through without going astray. They may not know of ways to resist peer-group pressure without feeling embarrassed; or they may have a limited repertory of ways to handle stress or make decisions; or the tangle of emotions common to adolescent years may be too confusing to steer through.

Sometimes what appears to be misbehavior arises from an unrelated problem the child is having. If you look beyond the apparent discipline problem, you often find the child is facing a difficult situation and just can't cope. Better, then, to help him overcome the underlying problem than to address just the misbehavior.

For instance, say your eleven-year-old is teasing his brother. You size up the situation and recognize that he's really frustrated with a math problem he can't solve or anxious about a math test he has coming up. Helping him with his math will allow him to return to his homework and leave his brother alone.

The mother of fourteen-year-old Barbara found a note that showed the teenager was depressed and thinking about suicide. The mother knew enough about her daughter to realize she'd been upset lately because her father drank too much and was then demanding, highly critical, and unable to listen to or pay much attention to Barbara. Instead of reacting directly to the depression and the implied threat of suicide, Barbara's mother decided to talk to her about coping with a father who drinks. She bought Barbara a booklet on the subject and after asking her to read it, talked with her about how difficult it is for a teenager to live with an alcoholic father.

Her mother suggested several ways Barbara could cope more successfully. They were not necessarily easy to come up with, so her mother did some reading and talked with a substance-abuse counselor first. Then she told Barbara about a group at her school designed to help teens cope with a substance-abusing parent. She also offered to help her find a therapist to talk to if she wanted that. During their conversation, she repeatedly advised Barbara not to take her father's drinking personally, blame herself, or view herself as being responsible for helping him solve his drinking problem. Afterward, Barbara hugged her mother and gave her a genuine "Thanks for understanding, Mom."

Young people often start misbehaving when they are stuck on a problem they can't resolve. It may be as simple as a math problem, or as complex as a father or mother who is an addict. It may be a boyfriend or girlfriend who wants to break up, a friend who is pregnant, a divorced parent who doesn't call often enough, or a teacher who picks on the young person. Whatever the problem, young people may need assistance in getting over a conflict, hurt, or disappointment.

It's important that the parent understand the real nature of the difficulty and offer coping strategies that are relevant and truly helpful to the child.

Useful coping strategies could include suggestions about how to deal with peer pressure about drinking. It may be helpful for your child to practice ways to say no ("No, thanks, I don't drink"; "I don't like the taste"; "I'm allergic"; "If you're my friend, why are you pressuring me to do something I don't want to do?"), or for you to suggest alternatives to alcohol: "Some people drink fruit punch, ginger ale, or sparkling water at a party because it looks like a mixed drink and then no one bothers them."

Suggesting good study techniques may help children get through difficult school subjects: "The preview, question, read, reflect, and review method is very effective. First you preview the material, reading headings and getting a sense of the overall content. Then you ask yourself questions you want the material to answer. Then read, looking for the answers to your question. Take notes of the most important points, and reflect on each section after you read it. Finally, review your notes after you've finished the entire reading assignment."

Advice on how to handle a first traffic ticket may be welcomed: "You might show up for your court date and ask the judge to give you six months to prove you are a capable and careful driver."

Poor coping strategies are those that dictate to a young person ("You have to start thinking of yourself"), employ generalities and few specifics ("Grow up and accept it like a man"), or are too simplistic or contain advice the child has heard before ("Just say no when they offer you drugs").

I know a fifteen-year-old boy who had started getting into fights at school and being sarcastic to a teacher—something highly unusual for him. His parents first thought of grounding him for the recent rash of behavior problems at school, but decided to look into the situation a little more before taking action.

When they talked to his friends and to his school counselor and teachers, they began to understand that Bryan was really upset because he wanted out of learning-disability classes, which he had been in for almost six years. He no longer wanted to be viewed as a handicapped person. He finally wanted to be "like everyone else."

Instead of punishing Bryan for school misbehavior, his

parents approached him and suggested there were probably reasons why he was acting out of character. If he could share some of his feelings about school, perhaps they could help out. Bryan was able to tell them enough that they could put the pieces of the puzzle together.

They recognized he needed coping strategies to get out of learning-disabilities classes and be more successful in regular classes. His parents suggested that he start by speaking directly to his school counselor. "Why not be up front with her and tell her you no longer want to be in LD classes?" they said.

They continued to offer other ways of dealing with this problem. They helped him map out a step-by-step plan for switching classes and reviewed with him what he would have to do differently in regular classes. He would, they said, have to consider changing his study methods and they talked with him about his major study deficiencies.

Addressing a second underlying problem, they recommended that he become more involved with school organizations and activities to help him to feel more popular and to fit in with his peers.

Specific coping strategies for stress can teach young people relaxation techniques; for problems giving speeches, a course in public speaking; for study problems, a book on effective study skills; for depression, exercise, involvement in community affairs, a change in diet, or psychotherapy.

7. Offer Encouragement

As parents, we understand that kids make mistakes and get into trouble sometimes not because they are bad people, but because they are young, inexperienced, and often impulsive. Knowing these things, we not only have to give them a certain amount of leeway, but we also need to give them a lot of encouragement.

Children need an indication from us that they are doing better, improving, or getting close to what we expect. They especially need encouragement when there has been a problem, mistake, or misbehavior.

It is easy to give children encouragement when they are living up to what we want from them. It is harder when they are failing. But that's when they most need our support. The last thing a child needs to be reminded of is how far short of perfect he is. When we give encouragement in such situations, we are saying to a young person, "I haven't given up on you at all, and in fact I'm proud of how much better you've been doing."

Encouragement can be an effective technique with children or teenagers who generally strive to do well and feel bad when they let down their parents. They don't need criticism because they already give that to themselves. Blake is an example of this.

Blake has been worried about his report card for two weeks; he remembers what his parents said about his last grades. Since then he has really tried, but he is worried about his science grade. He may not even pass the class, and if he doesn't he is sure his parents will "kill" him. Today the report card arrived and he brought it in from the mailbox and handed it to his parents. They looked it over gravely and then his father spoke: "Nice job on your grades, son. I especially like the way you raised your algebra and English grades. Your citizenship marks have improved and I can see by your effort grade in science that you've really tried hard. If you keep working this hard, you're going to get a mark in there you'll feel proud of."

Blake breathed a sigh of relief and whispered a silent prayer of thanks that his father was so positive. He told himself he would continue to work harder. That night before going to sleep he thought of another way he could improve his science work.

Criticism of young people who are already hard on themselves serves only to increase their anxiety without any appreciable gain in their ability to strive harder. If they have been putting forth effort, giving recognition for their attempts to improve is more likely to help them to redouble their efforts.

A risk of using encouragement as a technique is that a child may believe you are condoning a misbehavior or that you feel he has made enough improvement. If a fourteen-year-old has skipped school and you say, "Well, at least that's the only time you've skipped this semester," the implication may be it's okay to cut classes at least once a semester.

On the other hand, a teen who has worked hard to cut down on truancies from classes deserves encouragement. It should be given at the appropriate time, however. That might best be when he brings home a report card that shows few or no truancies or right after he lets you know that he was able to say no when a friend suggested skipping algebra.

8. Show Interest

A technique much like encouragement is showing interest. Children frequently need someone to show some interest in their work hobbies or projects. If your daughter's interest in homework is flagging and it looks as if she may give up or watch television instead of completing it, asking questions about her work may revive her own interest.

Similarly, when your son is struggling to complete a job, chore, or task at home, showing that you like the job he's doing, have questions about the way he's doing it, or appreciate his accomplishment can keep him involved (and often out of trouble) until the job is completed.

Rod returned to high school after an auto accident and a serious concussion. He was not a great student before the accident, but now he had something to prove. He wanted to prove to himself and to others that he could be a better student and that his head injury would have no lasting effects.

His father talked to his son's doctor and his rehabilitation nurse and understood that Rod would need a lot of assistance in the coming months. Because of this his father decided to show as much interest as possible.

Rod's father had some background in journalism and had published several articles and essays, so he saw an opportunity to give Rod plenty of support in his journalism class in particular. Several times a week, Rod's father asked about his journalism assignments and read over his son's articles, sometimes offering suggestions and almost always asking questions. The questions motivated Rod to talk about his latest article and how he developed the lead.

Rod ate up this attention and worked harder to impress his father. The interest served to redouble Rod's efforts to bounce back from a situation that could have been a handy excuse to give up on school.

Showing interest, like all the other discipline techniques in this chapter, does not harm kids, usually gives them a needed boost, and generally makes both parents and children feel better and more successful.

Summary

The following discipline techniques assist young people to learn new lessons and handle problems in different ways.

- Ask think questions.
- Tell stories that make a point.
- Role play.
- Make an interpretation.
- Hold a post-event discussion.
- Teach coping strategies.
- Offer encouragement.
- Show interest.

NINE

Techniques That Encourage Desired Behavior

EVERY CHILD does things that are positive, appropriate, and desired by her parents. No child, not even the worst or most poorly behaved youngster, is bad all the time. One of the things you want to do as a parent is to increase the behavior you like. How do you do that? This chapter offers guidance.

Some parents won't consider the techniques described in this chapter as discipline. That's because they are all positive responses—not to behavior you want to change or stamp out, but to behavior you see as good and desirable.

Catch them doing good may be a cliché, but it remains sage advice—particularly for parents. In fact, it is essential if the techniques in this chapter are to be used appropriately.

School surveys show that for every positive comment children hear from teachers, they hear three to five negative ones. If that's true in the classroom, I'd bet the ratio of bad to good comments at home is also weighted to the negative. Think of what it does to you as an adult when all you hear is criticism.

Now imagine how devastating the same situation could be for a child. All of us, but especially children, respond well to positive feedback and to encouraging attention. When children are given such feedback, they work hard to get more.

1. Give Praise and Attention

All children need attention. It's another overused piece of advice that counselors, therapists, and child-care experts toss around freely with parents.

"Mrs. Jones, your daughter needs more of your attention. That's the problem."

"I think the reason why Bobby gets into trouble is that he's looking for attention."

It may be true that some parents need to give more attention to their children, or that certain children and teenagers act up in order to get attention. But what does this mean exactly?

Attention giving means focusing on your child's behavior so that you're aware, generally, of what she's feeling and thinking; and being responsive so that she knows someone is there for her.

This is very easy to do with an infant; most parents are adept at it and enjoy the time they spend with an infant. Every behavior and developmental advance of your baby is attended to as if no other child had ever been so unique or wonderful. There is direct eye contact, smiling, cooing, and verbal praise for the child's first words, first teeth, or first steps.

While you spend time devoted exclusively to your child, you give plenty of physical affection and verbal feedback. What you are doing—not with any conscious intent to change or direct behavior, but just because it's enjoyable—is giving the child attention that serves to teach her about communication, love, trust, and feeling good about herself.

Every time you give that kind of attention to your child,

you make it more likely she will want more of this attention and will do whatever it is that got her in that spotlight in the first place.

Giving praise is one form of giving attention. By saying something positive about an action you like, you let your child know what behavior you desire.

When Sammy brings home a report card that shows he raised his social studies grade from a D to a C, his father responds with sincere praise: "Sammy, you raised your grade. You worked hard and I'm proud of you."

In another family, Kristin frequently puts up a fuss about going to bed. One night she went to bed the first time her parents announced it was bedtime. Pleasantly surprised, her parents didn't waste the opportunity to praise her. Both parents tucked her in and her mother said as she stroked Kristin's arm, "Honey, we're really proud of you. You went to bed tonight when we asked you to. That's really great. We love you. Good night, sleep tight."

To use praise effectively, parents have to notice appropriate and desired behavior. I have so often seen parents overlook the positive things their children do while jumping all over them for the bad things. I think the reason for this is that mothers and fathers expect good behavior and therefore make no big deal of it when it occurs.

To make sure praise works, though, you have to be on your guard to catch children doing well. Then shower them with sincere praise and flattering comments.

"You got dressed all by yourself. Good job!"

"You took out the trash for Mrs. Snelling next door. I'm really happy that you help her out."

"You helped your sister with that algebra problem she couldn't do. What a kind, thoughtful thing to do!"

If you want kids to do good things often, then never let it go unnoticed or uncommented on when they do what you want. Take advantage of these opportunities to increase the likelihood they will continue.

"Thanks for hanging up your jacket. You're a big help!"

"I appreciate your taking the time to clean your plate and knife after you fixed yourself a sandwich."

"I really like it when you get your homework done so quickly."

It is advisable to avoid directing attention to things you wish a child wouldn't do or behavior that drives you crazy. Make mention only of the actions that are desired, and postpone comment on unwanted behavior for another time. It's tempting to yell, scream, criticize, blame, or punish when your children are quarreling with each other. Better, however, to ignore that and wait until they are playing well together to heap on some praise. "What good kids I have! I'm really lucky to have two great kids who know how to play well together."

In praising children, be sure that how you word your praise fits the needs and the personality of each child. Get to know the best way to word your praise so each child "eats it up." One child may like praise that is gushy and lavish. Another child may need to be told how mature and grown up she is. Yet another may like being reminded she is Mom's or Dad's little helper. Another may respond to being told how independent or considerate she is. Some children like to be touched or hugged while you are praising and some may not like any physical affection.

Always use praise during or immediately after the behavior you want to see continue; don't wait an hour or a day, do it now. This is not only good psychology (because the closer to an event, the more easily the child makes a connection between the praise and her behavior), it also ensures you don't forget.

Make sure, too, that your words of praise are descriptive.

Instead of just saying, "Thanks, Bob," say, "Wow! Bob, you cleaned up the whole garage so fast! I don't know how you did a neat job so quickly!" When you are specific and descriptive, it helps kids know exactly what they have to do in the future to get more praise.

Be sure your praise is sincere. You don't want your children to question whether you mean it or not. If you're not used to giving praise, however, you may find that at first it comes out sounding (or at least feeling to you) somewhat fake or phony. Usually, with more practice, you'll find that you can get better at it, so you can include such positive words as great, wonderful, terrific, excellent, outstanding, marvelous, and so on.

Don't use the same words or catch phrases every time. Instead, vary your praise. Say "I appreciate your brushing the dog" one time and another time say "Thanks for remembering to brush the dog's hair. You're a big help."

Praise can have a powerful effect on the behavior of children. Praise encourages good behavior, helps build children's self-esteem, and improves your effectiveness as a parent. Praise teaches kids to do what you want, and using it well not only makes for happier children but fosters a stronger and more harmonious family life.

2. Use Suggestive Praise

Suggestive praise is a way of using praise to tell children what you want from them while also letting them know what you don't want.

Let me give an example. Rachel is a twelve-year-old who does not like to do her household chores. One of those chores is to scrape off the dishes, place them in the dishwasher, turn on the dishwasher, and then clean the kitchen three nights a week following dinner. Often, however, she complains and picks an argument with her mother, which frequently delays her starting the chore.

One night, after only one reminder from her mother, Rachel began to scrape the plates—without any hassle or the usual complaining. As Rachel was wiping down the countertop and placing the last pan in the cupboard, her mother entered the kitchen and said, "Rachel, what a nice job! And it was wonderful to have you start right in on the dishes without our usual hassle. I appreciate that!"

The key words in the comment are *without* and the phrase that follows. In using praise, the words should be positive, descriptive, and sincere. Negative and inappropriate behavior should be ignored. With suggestive praise, though, you still praise a child's efforts or behavior in descriptive ways ("I was just so pleased to hear that you took the time to visit Grandmother and help her paint her house . . ."). But you also add a descriptive comment about the behavior that you want to decrease (". . . without asking her for money or a gift").

In effect, what suggestive praise does is to let young people know both what you want them to do ("Thanks for hanging up your jacket . . .") and what you don't want them to do (". . . instead of throwing it on the couch").

Using suggestive praise requires that you add such phrases as instead of, for not, and without. Other examples using these phrases are:

- "Great job! You ate your dinner without spilling your milk once."
- "You went to bed on time last night instead of making excuses about not being tired."
- "Thank you for coming straight home from school without stopping to play with your friends."
- "I appreciate it that you did not complain when I asked you to go with us to visit your grandmother."

Parents who are more accustomed to criticizing than praising their children sometimes prefer suggestive praise to praise alone. When they begin learning to use praise properly, they wonder how and when they can let kids know what they should *not* be doing. Suggestive praise gives parents an opportunity to do that, but in a constructive, helpful way.

Give suggestive praise to children when they are not misbehaving. It is always important to know what you are promoting or reinforcing. Like praise, this technique must be descriptive in that it specifically tells kids what you like them to do and also what you are glad they are not doing. And, of course, it must be sincere. There is a better chance your children will listen to your suggestive praise if you vary how you say it each time.

It's easier to win the trust and confidence of your children if you combine physical affection with suggestive praise. The words are important, but so are the physical indications that you love them.

3. Give Rewards and Privileges

Like praise and suggestive praise, rewards and privileges are specific consequences for specific desired actions. Successful parents reward their children for behavior they want repeated. Whether it is a simple pat on the back for hitting a home run or a spontaneous gift in recognition of a job well done, giving rewards and privileges is a way of linking good behavior with the pleasure of parental recognition.

As many studies show, giving rewards has a powerful influence on behavior. It can be used effectively to encourage desirable behavior and to help solve behavior problems. It's also a positive technique in that it helps children build a healthy self-image and fosters self-control.

Even simple, inexpensive rewards can influence behavior.

They can include gold stars, pennies, candy, a small toy, or more time with a parent; or they can be as expensive as a new telephone, a new baseball glove, or a shiny new bike. Rewards and privileges encourage children to try again or continue doing what you like.

Privileges, like more tangible rewards, express your pleasure with their behavior. Privileges include letting children do new or different things, take on new or greater responsibilities, have fun in new ways, spend time with friends, or spend extra time alone with a parent. This technique is easy to incorporate into your ordinary activities. You can adapt some of the nice things you already do for your kids to its use.

For example, suppose you buy all of your son's clothes, and lately he has been asking for a new pair of expensive sneakers like the ones his favorite NBA basketball star wears. You know that you will break down and get them sooner or later. You can use the purchase as an opportunity to reinforce positive behavior if you handle it like this:

"Tim, since you've been extra kind to your brother this week by playing with him and letting him join your friends' ball game, I thought I'd buy you that pair of high tops you've been asking for. Let's go tonight and get them, okay?"

Privileges can be used in the same way. "Alice, your father and I are so proud of you for getting to the bus stop on time each morning that we're going to let you go out with your boyfriend on Saturday night."

Older children and teenagers are always thrilled to get new privileges, freedom, or responsibilities. Younger children like to spend extra time with one or both parents or to stay up later.

When you alternate privileges with rewards, and both include praise and physical affection, you have a powerful combination that is extremely likely to lead your child to continue doing those things you desire.

When a girl I know was three years old, she got into the

habit of waking up late at night and coming into her parents' bed. This was cute the first few times, but the girl's parents wanted their bed to themselves. There was nothing wrong with her bed and her frilly bedroom. They decided to try a reward approach to induce her to sleep the whole night in her own bed.

They made up a simple chart listing the days of the week and told their daughter the following: "We've made a chart for you. This tells us how many nights you sleep in your own room all night. That's what Mommy and Daddy want: We want you to sleep all night in your own bed. If you sleep the whole night in your bed, you get to put a gold star, like this one, on your chart in the morning."

The next morning the girl had not slept the whole night in her room, so she couldn't put a star on her chart. Her parents expressed disappointment because she missed out on a star but assured her she could paste a star the next morning "when you stay all night in your own bed." It took her three tries before she won a star, which she licked and pasted on the chart with glee. Within thirty days, the girl was putting stars on her chart nearly every day. By the end of the second month, she was sleeping in her own room six nights out of seven and the parents decided to abandon the reward program. There was no relapse. One of the important reasons the girl didn't go back to her old habits after the chart and gold star were abandoned was that the parents also used lots of praise and attention— suggestive praise and physical affection. The combination was so powerful, the girl liked all the positive attention she was getting and it wasn't worth it to go back to her old ways.

If it's a thirteen-year-old who's having a problem, gold stars aren't going to work. But a new bike, a baseball glove, a hockey game with Dad, a new pair of sneakers, or a bigger allowance could make the desired behavior occur more often.

A good time to use rewards and privileges is when your

child has done something difficult or out of the ordinary or has put forth some special effort.

Rewards and privileges work best when they are given during or immediately after the action you like. For instance, if your daughter has spent a week helping her grandmother when she was ill or your son has just lugged the garbage out for the trash pickup, your child should have a reward immediately. If four-year-old Darryl has gotten through a toy store without his usual tantrum, he should be rewarded before leaving the store, not several hours or two days later. His mother can buy him a small toy and say as they leave the store, "Darryl, you were so helpful in the store today and I liked the way you behaved so much, I want you to have this toy." Darryl will be able to associate this reward with his controlled behavior much better than if his mother waits until they get home. The longer the wait, the less effective a reward will be.

Rewards should never be given *before* a desired behavior or they become bribes. If the reward is given with the hope the task or behavior will be completed, then you are *not* teaching children that you appreciate the whole behavior. You may also be removing the youngster's motivation to complete the job. If you want Mary to finish her homework before she goes with her friend to the mall, don't give her the money you are going to give her for shopping before the last math problem is done. If she gets the money before the homework is completed, she may just say, "Gee, Mom, I'm tired of doing all this math Mr. Kim gave us. I guess I'll finish it when I get home." Then, when Mary gets home from the mall, "I'm so tired I'm going to bed. I'll bet we walked ten miles looking for a prom dress. I'll just get up early to do my homework tomorrow." Right!

Although rewards effectively reinforce positive behavior, they are *not* effective when it comes to stopping misbehavior. When you tell Jeremy that you'll give him a quarter if he'll stop jumping on the new couch, you're bribing, not rewarding.

Paying off a child in this case only teaches him how to extort. It would not be surprising for Jeremy to say later, "I'll do the dishes if you pay me" or "If you don't give me five bucks, I'm not going to do anything around here!" That's not what you want. You want to be in control of the rewards and not be held up by a bandit whom you also claim as a dependent on your income tax form. If your child says she will not go to school or do her chores unless you increase her allowance or allow her to go out on Saturday night, calmly explain that she will not get anything she asks for. You as the parent are in control. Whether it is a demand or a request, unless you approve, you do not give in.

To improve the efficiency of rewards and privileges, accompany them with a description of the desired behavior. The description tells your kids what they did to earn the reward. "Sandy, you came home from school on time today and I have your favorite dessert for dinner." The description also serves to let a child know how to behave in the future to make rewards more likely. "You did what Daddy asked when you picked up all your toys from the family room. Let's go out and fly the kite."

Positive, friendly, and encouraging words also serve to make rewards and privileges more effective. Instead of saying "Well, I guess you earned something for your hard work on the lawn today," be more positive: "I'm so delighted with the careful way you trimmed the hedge and the time you put in raking the dead leaves off the front lawn, I'm going to do something special for you. I'm getting you that new Huey Lewis tape you've wanted."

Rewards and privileges work better, too, if they are varied each time they are used. That keeps up young people's interest and makes them less likely to get bored with a discipline approach that is becoming old hat. Likewise, keep in mind what you know about your kids. Individualize your rewards and privileges so that they are truly appreciated. A teenager who doesn't like pop music won't get excited by the Huey Lewis tape, but might relish a new novel or a chance to pick the videocassette the family will watch this weekend.

Finally, rewards do not have to be expensive to be effective. Of course, for a high school graduation or other special occasion you might want to take your child and a friend to the best restaurant in town. Privileges that kids generally value include more time with friends, permission to have a friend stay over night, the right to stay up later, an extra hour of television watching, greater use of the family car, and more responsibility in the family.

4. Make Promises

Promises can work very effectively in conjunction with both rewards and privileges. By telling children ahead of time what they can do to earn rewards and privileges, parents encourage them to behave well or perform in a certain way in the future.

Promises motivate children and teenagers to put forth some effort, do a specific task, work hard, or continue present behavior. When you say, "If you continue to play quietly, I will take you to the playground at four o'clock," you are teaching a child to be independent and responsible. Matt, for instance, knows he can get his bike repaired if he does the dishes for two nights. That gives Matt the opportunity to make a mature and responsible decision about whether or not he will do the dishes.

You must follow through on promises or they'll quickly become ineffective. Failing to keep your word may undermine your use of rewards and privileges as well.

ALL THE TECHNIQUES discussed in this chapter are positive ones that help to reinforce what you want children to do or keep doing. Children do many things right, and when parents encourage them to continue doing those things, we are assisting children to be motivated and well behaved and to feel like worthwhile, appreciated human beings.

The positive and encouraging parenting skills—giving praise and attention, suggestive praise, rewards and privileges, and promises—are easier to use than punishments, have very little chance of producing negative side effects, and are most likely to make both children and parents feel good about themselves and each other.

Summary

Use these discipline techniques to reinforce desired and appropriate behavior.

- Give praise and attention.
- Use suggestive praise.
- Give rewards and privileges.
- Make promises.

T E N

Techniques That Correct Behavior

IN THIS CHAPTER and the next, I will describe ways of dealing with behavior you do not like or consider undesirable or inappropriate.

While you are teaching lessons and improving problem-solving abilities as described in chapter 8, or reinforcing desirable actions through techniques described in chapter 9, you will also want to put a stop to some of the things your kids do from time to time. Designed to correct behavior you view as negative, these techniques are useful with a variety of young people. They will be most effective if they are used in conjunction with the positive techniques discussed in the previous chapter.

1. Define Limits

Defining limits, as discussed in chapter 6, can help to prevent problems. But you can also use this technique after your child has misbehaved to stop or correct that misbehavior.

Defining limits means letting kids know what the rules, limits, and boundaries are. Young people frequently need to be told where they must stop. By defining a limit, you give kids stop signs and directions so they can apply the brakes to their behavior.

Suppose your sixteen-year-old stayed out an hour later than she said she would on an evening out with friends. This doesn't happen often, so you would like to avoid punishing her. Yet it concerns you because you don't want it to become a regular habit. One way to handle it is by going over the rules with her—in other words, defining the limits.

When you define the limits, you tell her what the rule is about coming in at night: "We want all of our children in the house by midnight." And you remind her what you expect of her: "We expect that you will be in by midnight unless you call and we okay your staying out later, or unless we all agree beforehand that you may stay out later."

Letting kids know the rules and limits through a frank and firm reminder tells them two things: (1) you are well aware that they have broken a rule; (2) you are serious about their keeping the rule.

Defining the limits is especially appropriate for teenagers who, as they strive for more independence and freedom, need to be reminded where the stop signs are.

Of course, defining limits will not correct or change all misbehavior. But it is a place to start. As I hope I have made clear in previous chapters, I don't believe all problem behavior is so serious or dangerous it calls for immediate correction. In fact, children and teenagers need the leeway to make and correct mistakes on their own. That's one way that we show our ultimate trust and faith in them and restrain ourselves from being constantly on the lookout for bad behavior and opportunities to inflict punishment.

A proper way to define the limits is to state the rule and make it clear how you want it followed. For instance, if your daughter tends to go overboard disciplining her younger brother, you can define the limits this way: "It is not your responsibility to deal with your brother's misbehavior. That's a parent's responsibility. I will deal with any problems he has."

No threats are implied and no other action need be taken at this time. If the child keeps making the same mistakes over again, stronger action might be taken. First, though, be sure your child knows exactly what rule was broken and what you expect.

2. Make a Contract

Many parents and family therapists find making a contract to be one of the most effective ways available to bring about behavior change. This technique involves a negotiated agreement between parent and child.

For example, Richard, a fourteen-year-old, was always complaining about the strict rules his parents made for him. He thought that he had to come home too early, wasn't allowed to have friends over often enough, and had to spend too much time doing homework. Another source of irritation was the rule about his hair. He couldn't wear his hair in the style he preferred—a style much longer and more flamboyant than his parents thought appropriate. They insisted on monthly haircuts and a conservative style.

The issue seemed unresolvable until Richard's parents learned in therapy about making contracts and decided to try it. They hoped that a contract would eliminate the regular arguments over haircuts and hairstyle.

They asked Richard if he would be willing to work out a written contract with them to try to eliminate problems over his hair. He seemed willing but was hesitant at first, wondering if this was just a way of forcing him to do something he didn't want to do. His parents explained that a contract was an agreement worked out between two parties and that neither side had to sign it until they concurred on all the terms. He agreed and the next night the negotiations began.

Several nights and several drafts later, Richard and his parents had a contract they could all live with. Each party had gotten something it wanted, while each also gave up something, too.

The contract between Richard and his parents read like this:

> I, Richard, agree to make my own appointments to get my hair cut. I will not let it hang down below my eyebrows or be longer than the collar of my shirt. I will wash it every day.
>
> We, Mr. and Mrs. Henry, agree to allow Richard to wear his hair in any style he pleases as long as he follows his part of this contract. We will not go to the barbershop with him. We also agree not to criticize his hairstyle or remind him about washing his hair, combing it, or getting haircuts.

Richard and his parents signed and dated the contract. The arguments between Richard and his parents stopped after the contract was made. A year later, he was not wearing his hair in an outrageous or "embarrassing" (to his parents) style. For both Richard and his parents, the contract was an unqualified success. Richard no longer had a reason to complain about his parents' rules about his hair.

Contracts between parents and children can be used to solve a variety of problems (some of which are certainly much more serious and significant than the hairstyle of their offspring). Some of the problem behaviors for which contracts can work include misuse of the family car, running away, truancy, failure to do school work, drug use, curfew violations, and poor attitude and behavior in the home.

For contracts to be successful, both parents and young people have to get something from the agreement. Also, neither side can feel coerced into agreeing to the final terms. If kids feel they have no choice, there's an excellent chance they won't live up to their end of the bargain. Many parents make an "agreement" with their kids by telling the kids what is expected and what the kids must do. In the end, if your kids don't agree to a contract, it won't work.

3. Assign Responsibility

Used appropriately, holding a misbehaving child accountable for his actions can help to correct behavior. This entails telling a child, "You are responsible for this problem." It's a confrontational technique that lets a young person know he should accept blame for a particular situation. This technique must be intended as a constructive analysis or evaluation of a problem or weakness rather than as a rebuke. Your goal is not to make the child feel chagrined but to make him accept responsibility for a problem or misbehavior. Here's an example.

Harold was a self-centered teenager who frequently demanded his own way. He had more conflicts with his mother than with his father, and his mother also gave in to Harold's demands more readily. One day, after he'd coerced his mother into taking him shopping for a new pair of jeans he "just had to have" that day, his father pointed out to Harold that he often didn't seem to consider his mother or her schedule in making demands.

Harold neither apologized nor acknowledged that what his father said was true. His father then attempted to make Harold aware of the problem he had in many relationships.

"Harold," he said, "your actions are responsible for disrupting things in this family. You often act as if you don't care about other's feelings and you generally lack consideration for their lives or needs. It is your responsibility to make changes in your behavior."

The goal of this technique is to correct an undesired behavior by enlightening the child about his responsibility for it.

It is a potentially dangerous technique because it can further damage an already fragile or bruised ego. Insecure young people will react as if reprimanded and become defensive and resentful.

The child who can best benefit from this technique is one who is willing to accept the guilt and will not blame someone else in turn. Instead, he will work hard to bring his behavior up to an acceptable level.

Mr. and Mrs. Gunther came to see me about some family problems. One of the problems concerned their sixteen-year-old daughter, Michelle. A good girl in many ways, Michelle achieved above-average grades, sang in the church choir, and had a part-time job in a flower shop. Yet she had this uncanny knack for waiting until the last minute to do things. This habit caused arguments between her parents.

"Take the business about her signing up for her SATs," her father explained to Mrs. Gunther in one of their frequent fights. "She waited until the last minute and then sprang it on us that we had to take her to the post office so the application could be postmarked by midnight."

What happens next? Her father tells Michelle it's her problem, and her mother defends Michelle, saying it's important they get the application in on time.

This type of scene occurred repeatedly. The specifics changed, but always Michelle was late, her father was angry, and her mother defended Michelle. God forbid that either parent might have better things planned when Michelle's emergency arose—that's what usually led to her parents' fights.

Her father might be tired, have a meeting scheduled, or just not feel like altering his schedule to suit his daughter. His wife saw him as being unreasonable.

I advised Mr. Gunther to stop fighting with his wife and place some responsibility where it belonged: on Michelle.

After the next incident, when Michelle "had" to be taken shopping on a Thursday night because she was going on a wilderness adventure with a school class the next morning and she "absolutely" had to have water purification tablets and waterproof matches, Mr. Gunther tried something different.

"Michelle," Mr. Gunther began, as he drove her to school the next morning, "you know I love you and I'm proud of everything you've accomplished. However, there are things you do I don't like very much. For instance, when you put things off until the last minute. When that happens, it puts the family in an uproar and your mother and I fight about your needs and demands.

"That is not the way I want things to continue in this family. Frankly, I think you would want things different, too. While you're gone on this camping trip, I wish you would give some thought to making some changes because you need to see that you continually put things off until the last minute, put unreasonable demands on your mother and me, and cause us to fight. I think you can handle your end of things in a more responsible way."

It would be difficult for Michelle or any other teenager to avoid getting this message. Mr. Gunther didn't ask how she felt about anything and wasn't subtle. Neither was he disrespectful or dictatorial. He was straightforward, placed the responsibility on her, and told her what he would like to see changed. That is an appropriate use of this technique.

There are many ways of using this technique inappropriately. The young person must not be scapegoated ("You're the problem in this family"), ridiculed ("You're always doing dumb things"), or attacked personally ("You're a selfish brat"). Instead, the parent's statements assigning responsibility should be objective and indicate the change that is sought.

This technique should be reserved for use with older children and adolescents. Children over ten years of age have better abstract thinking skills and may be more capable of understanding the point the parent is making without taking the parental remarks in such a way as to feel personally wounded.

THE DISCIPLINE techniques presented in this chapter are designed to solve existing problems or misbehavior, and the risks they pose vary. While assigning responsibility is not effective with all kids, making contracts can be used with a wide range of teenagers as well as with certain difficult youngsters. One of its strengths is that it generally increases communication within the family.

Summary

Discipline techniques that can help correct misbehavior are:

- Define limits.
- Make a contract.
- Assign responsibility.

ELEVEN

Techniques That Discourage Undesired Behavior

WHEN I TEACH parent training and discipline classes, I find this is the section parents await most eagerly. In this chapter, I discuss punishment techniques. While the parents in my classes are not necessarily malicious or overly punitive, they do tend to be more comfortable with punishments to stop their children's misbehavior than with preventive and positive techniques.

I'm not sure of the reasons for this. It could be that many of the parents who come to my classes grew up with punishment. More likely, though, it's because parents who seek out discipline classes have experienced repeated problems with a child and have come to believe nothing will work but punishment.

I hope it has been clear up to this point that I strongly believe the various discipline techniques previously described are the ones parents should rely on first—before they turn to punishments. It can't be emphasized too often that if you frequently use the techniques described in chapters 5 through 10, you seldom will have to resort to the techniques in this chapter.

The discipline skills in this chapter have a couple of important characteristics in common: (1) they are based on the idea that if your child is engaged in an undesired or inappropriate behavior, you can use a negative consequence to decrease or stop it; (2) they provide a suitable alternative to the ten worst discipline techniques described in chapter 2—techniques that are generally ineffective and harmful.

Punishment and negative techniques teach your child what *not* to do; the positive techniques in previous chapters are designed to teach kids what they *should* do.

If you come to depend on punishment, you will run the risk of being too harsh, punitive, and unloving with your child. Your kids are likely to see you as an ogre and want to avoid you.

Punishment used too often teaches kids something else: It teaches them what they can do to bug you and get you upset and rattled.

1. Ignore

The first skill you can use to decrease inappropriate and undesired behavior is to ignore the child. In chapter 7, I described the use of ignoring as a preventive discipline skill that helps foster self-control. As used in that way, ignoring allows a child to work out a problem and practice self-control without parental intervention.

Ignoring an action in order to decrease undesired behavior can be viewed as a punishment, although more accurately it is an extinction technique. That is, ignoring is a nonpunitive technique that gradually extinguishes a behavior.

This skill also plays a part in some of the other suggested disciplines in this book you may already be using. In describing praise and attention in chapter 9, I recommended that you refrain from responding to behavior you didn't want to reinforce and wait for behavior you wanted to continue. Similarly, I advised not to give rewards and privileges when your youngster was misbehaving. To *refrain* and to *wait* required you to *ignore;* so if you followed those suggestions, you've already begun to incorporate ignoring into your bag of discipline tricks. Even so, to use ignoring correctly, it is important to use it purposefully to stop specific misbehavior.

It is true that ignoring is one of the least punitive skills to be learned. But the interesting thing is that it is one of the most difficult discipline techniques for some parents to learn.

To parents with a particularly active history of intervening in every one of their children's problems or difficulties, it is strange to be told to keep out of their problems. One father expressed in words what a lot of others think about ignoring: "It goes against my nature," he said.

Some parents tell me ignoring their kids' misbehavior couldn't possible be effective, only to try it—sometimes with great reluctance—and later to report very good results. Mrs. Carlyle, for example, had a fifteen-year-old daughter who was on probation to the juvenile court for "home incorrigible behavior." As a consequence, Mrs. Carlyle was ordered to attend my parenting classes.

At first, Mrs. Carlyle was sure that the only thing that would help her daughter was punishment. "These problems have been going on for over a year," she explained. "That's why she's on probation. I've tried everything before and finally I had to go to the court."

She was assigned to use ignoring to deal with some of her daughter's disobedience. She was to ignore her daughter when the girl attempted to start an argument, made unreasonable demands, or sassed her mother.

Within four weeks, Mrs. Carlyle reported progress to the

class: "When I started ignoring those things that bothered me, she got upset. But then she just gradually stopped trying to bug me. I think a lot of the things she was doing were just to see me lose my temper."

The best way to use this technique is to withhold your attention from a child whose actions you wish to stop. "Won't my kids get the idea that they can get away with anything if I ignore bad behavior?" parents may legitimately ask. The answer is simple. You do not ignore *all* bad behavior. Ignoring should not be used to deal with dangerous or serious behavior. You use this discipline technique to handle minor or aggravating behavior. When you ignore minor misbehavior such as nighttime crying or whining, sibling squabbles, temper tantrums, and sarcastic or angry comments to parents, it is extremely effective.

Ignoring is the discipline of choice when your children are doing things that seem designed to get your attention, get your goat, or break down your resistance, such as pouting, whining, nagging, tattling, and swearing. For instance, seven-year-old Kimberly stood in the kitchen where her mother was preparing dinner and wailed, "Barbara won't play with me! She's mean. Do you know what she did? She hit me. I want you to tell her mother."

Kimberly's mother ignored her and did not respond with words, gestures, or a sympathetic look in her daughter's direction. She could see Kimberly out of the corner of her eye, however, and when she didn't look at Kimberly, the girl shrugged, turned, and walked toward the door. Five minutes later, when her mother looked for Kimberly through the kitchen window, she saw her and Barbara together in animated and cooperative play.

Ignoring will work well only if it is used with control and consistency. Be consistent by ignoring your child each time a particularly bothersome or annoying behavior occurs. This means that if you are trying to stop temper tantrums, you ignore each and every outburst of temper. Responding to some temper tantrums and not to others actually strengthens this kind of misbehavior. When you ignore troublesome behavior consistently and children figure out that it no longer works, they often give it up.

Ignoring means exactly that: pay *no* attention. There can be no staring, glaring, warnings, "tsking" or other verbal cues, or body language suggesting that you are troubled or otherwise notice the behavior. Showing any kind of response may reinforce the negative behavior rather than weaken it.

When you begin ignoring a problem in order to decrease it, you should expect the behavior to get worse at first. Children sometimes work harder to get your attention when they sense that it is being cut off. Generally, if you are consistent, the behavior will begin to occur less frequently.

You may need to do something to help yourself *not* respond at times. When a crying child or one in the throes of a temper tantrum raises the volume or intensifies the annoying behavior, it's difficult not to worry that the child will make herself sick, hurt herself, or react in some way that requires your attention and protection.

To help prevent yourself from intervening, you should have some plan in mind about how you will distract yourself. Many parents simply leave the room. Others count to ten, talk to their spouse or a friend, do some exercises, or read a book— literally anything that will keep them busy and keep their minds on something else. In the beginning, when you are first trying to be less of an active intervener, you can expect that it will be difficult to remain uninvolved.

Ignoring is more effective if you give praise, attention, encouragement, rewards, privileges, or suggestive praise after the misbehavior has stopped. For instance, you could say,

"Great! You stopped that temper tantrum all by yourself. I'm proud of you." Or, if you use suggestive praise, you might say, "You stopped fighting with your sister and began playing nicely with her without my having to say anything to you. Good for you!"

Children go beyond just annoying and minor misbehavior. While you can choose to ignore actions that have no potentially dangerous consequences, there will be others that may be quite the opposite. For dangerous or serious behavior—for example, hitting another child with a baseball bat, stealing, or running away—do not choose this discipline technique. Instead, select a more appropriate technique from the ones that follow.

2. Withhold Friendliness

The second discipline technique designed to bring about obedience is withholding friendliness. By threatening to withhold your love and affection, or by actually not being loving, warm, or friendly, you can stop misbehavior.

This is a simple technique, simply used. When a child is not obedient, the parent becomes distant and does not respond to the child in a friendly, loving manner.

Once a parent has set up a loving relationship with a child, this technique can be used to influence and change behavior. Most children wish to retain their parents' friendship and affection. When that is withdrawn, kids feel they have lost favor and will attempt to regain it by pleasing the parent. The implied threat of loss of love is very powerful with many children who feel close to their mother or father.

This technique, however, can be used successfully only when the parent and child have a genuinely loving relationship. And it certainly has some risks. Parents who rely heavily on this method are likely to foster dependency and oversensitivity in their children. However, as illustrated in the following story, this does not have to happen.

Jamie and his sister, Emily, were spending the afternoon with their mother. They had all looked forward to this time and were having fun; there was considerable warmth and good-natured kidding going on between them as they planned the rest of the afternoon.

When it came time to decide where they would eat, a snag developed. Jamie insisted that Burger King was the best place to go, but Emily said that Wendy's was the "very best" place to eat. Soon, Jamie and Emily were arguing. Their mother, unhappy with the turn of events, gave them both a frown as they continued to argue about the best place to eat. She kept driving in silence, but her scowl and her silence seemed to lower the temperature in the car by several degrees. Emily was the first to note the chilly atmosphere.

"You're making Mom mad," she told her brother.

"Am not!" he insisted. "You are!"

"She doesn't like it when we're fighting, Jamie," replied Emily, making her pronunciation of *Jamie* sound like a bad word. "I'm not going to fight about this anymore. If you want to go to Burger King, it's okay by me."

"All right," said Jamie, stealing a glance at his mother and not at all happy about his victory. His mother's face was impassive as she watched the traffic.

Everyone was quiet for several minutes before Jamie tried to break the ice by warily asking their mother about her work. It wasn't long before everyone was engaged in a cheery conversation and the temperature in the car was noticeably warmer.

The father in another family expressed his displeasure and threatened the withdrawal of his friendliness in a more direct way: "I don't like what you're doing, Robert," he would say to his son. His expression, his words, and the tone of his voice made it very clear to Robert that if he wanted his friendly father back, he had better stop doing what his father didn't like and do something that pleased his father.

This technique tells your child that a behavior is not approved. It should be reserved for situations and actions that require something other than ignoring.

There should be no confusion about the reason for your withdrawal of love and approval. Your child should not believe you disapprove of her in general. It should be connected to the behavior that is undesirable or inappropriate so that the child knows her behavior has brought disapproval. Once a change occurs or the child understands why there has been a change in her parent's friendliness, the parent must revert to loving and affectionate ways. Give praise and attention soon afterward to let the child know that she is still loved.

A young person may not understand why the friendliness has been withdrawn. If the child asks, give a short explanation. "I don't like it when you swear at Mommy" is an example of a short, clear explanation. Another is: "I'm unhappy with you when you don't follow our rules."

Do not impose excessive guilt or add lengthy explanations of the reasons for your unhappiness. The question is not an opportunity for a lecture, but the signal that the child may truly not understand why her mother or father is displeased with her. The question can be answered in a straight, clear, and short manner.

3. Impose a Time-out

Imposing a time-out is placing a child in a dull and non-stimulating area for a period of time following misbehavior. Children can be told to sit or stand in a corner, sit on a stair step, or sit on a chair in a room in which they normally do not play. This is a punishment that can be used for a variety of inappropriate behaviors including hitting, screaming, fighting, or talking back.

One of the advantages of this technique is that it is effective with more serious misbehaviors. In addition, it is immediate and brief. You can quickly put a stop to an unwanted activity, give punishment, end the punishment, and switch to a positive skill (such as praising a new desired behavior) all in the span of five to ten minutes.

What is particularly appealing to parents and child-care specialists alike is that this punishment is not harsh, is very humane, and doesn't usually cause parents or kids to be upset with each other.

To use time-out properly, first decide whether a misbehavior requires this technique or is better ignored. If it is a relatively serious behavior (say, breaking a sibling's toy or deliberately breaking a dish as opposed to your garden variety falling-on-the-floor-and-crying temper tantrum), then something more than ignoring is called for. In general, this technique should be considered for misbehavior involving aggressive, destructive, and defiant actions.

It is important, as it is with most punishment, to use time-out during or immediately after the misbehavior. The quicker you use this technique the better it will effect an association between the unwanted behavior and the time-out. If you intervene during the misbehavior, you can stop it and punish at the same time.

In using this technique, the parent first points out the misbehavior and then states the consequence: "You disobeyed by hitting. You must go to time-out." The first time it is used, the child will be told where to sit or stand, and perhaps the length of time she is to remain in time-out.

One of the problems parents encounter when they try to call time-out during serious misbehavior is that the child is uncooperative. A child out of control is not likely to walk meekly to the corner when you announce "Go to your time-out spot." Sometimes it is necessary to physically direct the youngster to the designated place. You can do this fairly easily with a preschooler, but it becomes more difficult as children get older and bigger. Taking a child firmly by the upper arm—without anger, pinching, or hurtful force—you can direct her to the time-out place. Do not be timid about this maneuver. Instead, you need to be firm enough so that she can't shake you off, run away, or otherwise wriggle out of your grasp.

If the child is so angry or out of control that physical directing does not work, you will have to be patient and read on to learn other punishment techniques that might apply.

The place designated for time-out should be uninviting, dull, and without entertainment value. There should be nothing to play with there. This is why many parents choose a corner of some room in the house. If a corner is your choice, it should be one without pictures or interesting wallpaper. This is also why the child's bedroom, a place where many kids these days have not only toys but TVs, stereos, and computers, should not be designated for time-out.

The reasons for this dullness should be obvious. What you don't want is for the time-out to be fun or entertaining. It is expected that time in this place will be punishment and not amusement.

That's also why time-outs should be brief. Even the child who hates time-out will find something to do to amuse herself if the time-out period is too long. Most people, confined to a dull place, will eventually find something to do to keep from being bored or going crazy. Children are no different. Too long in time-out and they will study the designs in the wallpaper, count the holes in the ceiling tile, daydream, or go to sleep.

As a general rule, time-out should not be much longer than about one minute for each year of age. For a preschooler of four years, time-out should last about three to five minutes. For active youngsters, particularly on a sunny day when their friends are all playing outside, three minutes might seem like an eternity.

Moderate punishments are usually more effective than more severe punishments. Therefore, even for a young teenager, fifteen minutes should be sufficient. It is not the length of time in time-out that makes it effective but the certainty that a particular action will result in a time-out. If you are attempting to eliminate a repeated misbehavior, it is more important to place the child in time-out every time the offending behavior occurs than to increase the length of time-out.

To make time-out more effective, keep your attention to a minimum while it lasts. As you announce time-out, make a brief statement about the problem behavior and the punishment, but that's all. For instance, you might say, "Dwayne, you cannot hit your father. You will have to go to time-out for five minutes."

Nothing else needs to be said, no matter what else Dwayne says or how he complains about the unfairness of this punishment, how mean you are, or why he is really innocent of the charges against him. You do not have to discuss time-out or his problem behavior at this time.

As already indicated, if your child argues or refuses to go to time-out, you can firmly direct her there. What you must avoid is giving her a lot of attention. If she finds she can get attention by acting up, the behavior will continue. Therefore, the less said the better.

A scenario with time-out should go something like this:

MOTHER: "Jennifer, you pushed Tommy into the swimming pool. That is dangerous and against our rules. You will have to sit in the living room for the next seven minutes."

JENNIFER: "But, Mom, he pushed me first!"

MOTHER: (Says nothing and points to the house.)

JENNIFER: "Mom, how come I have to stop swimming? (She starts to cry.) It isn't fair. (She continues to stand by the side of the pool.)

MOTHER: "Seven minutes in time-out and your seven minutes begin when you're seated in the living room."

JENNIFER: "I don't want to stop swimming!" (Mother holds her by the arm and walks her toward the house. In the house, she silently directs her to sit down. She checks her watch.)

Seven minutes later:

MOTHER: "Okay, Jennifer, your seven minutes are up. You can go back to the swimming pool now."

JENNIFER: "All right."

MOTHER: "If you don't push children into the pool, you won't have to come back to time-out. Okay?"

JENNIFER: "Okay."

There is no reason to say anything else before, during, or after time-out. You do not have to criticize the child's behavior or tell her how disappointed you are. However, once the child's time is up and you let her return to her previous activities, try to quickly find her doing what you appreciate so you can give her praise or attention. This will help to make time-out even more effective. By doing this, of course, you are letting her know the kind of behavior you do like.

If you have trouble keeping track of the time, use a timer or stopwatch. Children should not be kept in time-out longer than their designated time. Also, if a youngster is acting up, crying, or refusing to go to time-out, calmly tell her that time-out begins when she is quiet and in the designated spot.

You can teach appropriate behavior by again explaining, when time-out is over, why she was placed in time-out in the first place: "May, I want to remind you that you were put in time-out because you threw your food at dinner. I want you to remember that throwing food is wrong."

Finally, do not apologize for using time-out or do other things to lessen—or make more palatable for the child—the effects of punishment. Do *not* say: "I'm sorry you have to come in the house while the other children are having cake and ice cream, but . . ." And do *not* give her something to do—like keeping a stack of magazines near the time-out chair—while she's in time-out.

4. Remove Rewards and Privileges

In chapter 9 I explained the use of rewards, privileges, and promises to reinforce or strengthen a desired or appropriate behavior. If you want to diminish or stop misbehavior, you take away some of the same rewards and privileges.

Parents typically already know about this discipline skill because most of us have used grounding and confining a child to her room as a punishment. Those are specific examples of removing a reward or privilege.

As most parents know, removing a reward, privilege, or tangible item the young person already has and enjoys tends to be effective. This technique, like time-out, can be used to deal with serious rule infractions, particularly with an adolescent.

Sometimes time-out will be the better way to deal with undesired behavior; at other times, you may decide that removing a reward or privilege will work better. Like all other punishments mentioned in this book, taking away something teaches young people what they must not do. And, like other punishments, there are rules for the most powerful use of the technique.

The quicker you use this technique following an undesired behavior, the better the chance it will work. If you can invoke it during the behavior you don't like, so much the better. The problem of waiting ("Wait until your father comes home and he will deal with this, young man!") is that in the interim children may act up again or perhaps do something you really appreciate. If you then punish by taking something away, it could cause confusion about what they are being punished for.

It is essential that the reward or privilege taken away be valued by the child. Parents should know their children's likes and dislikes well enough to know what they enjoy or highly prize.

If you have a youngster who doesn't often play with other children, it would be relatively meaningless to restrict her play with friends. But take away the privilege of using the telephone from most fifteen-year-old girls and you have caused a major crisis. Some children enjoy playing video games, others like to go out with friends, still others enjoy having a TV in their room. The reward or privilege that has meaning should be the one removed.

It is important that the value of the reward or privilege taken away be somewhat equivalent to the degree of severity of the problem behavior. You don't, for instance, take away a major privilege (playing baseball on a summer traveling league) for a relatively minor infraction of the rules (forgetting to bring the trash cans in from the curb).

Young people are more likely to accept and learn from the punishment if it is fair and related to the offense.

A girl who spends too much time on the phone tying up the line so no one else can make telephone calls can probably understand if her phone privileges are curtailed or removed temporarily. Similarly, a boy who comes home late from playing with his friends is more likely to accept a punishment of not being able to play with his friends for a day than having his baseball card collection taken away for a week.

Removing a reward or privilege should be a temporary rather than permanent punishment. Like time-out, it should not be too severe. It is a common mistake for parents to ground kids or take away something they value for too long. Joe, a fifteen-year-old boy I worked with, stayed out too late. As a punishment, his father took his CB radio away for several months. One of Joe's favorite activities was to talk on the CB with people around his state. However, once he realized that he would not be getting his CB back soon, he learned to live without it. After he learned to compensate for this loss by developing new activities, any lesson value in taking away his CB was gone. Instead, Joe viewed his father as mean and arbitrary.

Some parents forget how long they have told their child the restriction or removal would last. Moreover, when parents over-react and remove a reward or privilege for a long period ("You're grounded to the house for this whole semester"), they frequently feel guilty or have second thoughts about the punishment. Consequently, it is better to state a short or moderate period of removal of a reward or privilege. You are less likely to forget the length of the punishment or to give in out of guilt. Punishments that are consistent and fair tend to work better.

Kids I've seen in therapy who have been given excessive punishments with this technique come to convince themselves, and not infrequently their parents, that the punishment doesn't matter, that it doesn't bother them. A short-term punishment leaves open the possibility that the young person will try to avoid the same punishment in the future.

Vary what you take away or remove. In this way, again, children will not get used to its absence and find something else to take its place. When this happens, that punishment is no longer effective. If you repeatedly take away a girl's bike, chances are that sooner or later she'll take up skateboarding or borrow a friend's extra bike.

When you tell a child she is going to lose a certain reward or privilege, be sure that you follow through. If you fail to follow through, instead of learning that she should stop doing what you dislike, the child learns that you don't mean what you say.

Don't let tears or promises to do better interfere with your resolve to follow through with a punishment. By backing down when a youngster appears sad, contrite, or willing to change, you teach only that tears and promises absolve her from punishment. You may be increasing the tears and promises when she gets caught—not decreasing the misbehavior.

Finally, avoid the temptation to remove rewards and privileges too often. It's easy to do if you're trying to change a number of undesirable habits. However, using this punishment too frequently reduces its effectiveness.

Alternate not only the rewards and privileges you use, but also the kinds of punishment you use. Many parents, feeling themselves losing control over their increasingly independent teenagers, panic and invoke this punishment to try to maintain at least a sense of control and effectiveness. However, overusing the removal of rewards and privileges can alienate teenagers just as much as being too critical or too sarcastic can.

Here are two stories that illustrate the inappropriate and appropriate use of this technique.

Sara, a tall fourteen-year-old, had gradually become more disrespectful to her mother. When she got angry with her mother, which was often, she would yell at her, swear, and call her names. Sara frequently yelled "Shut up!" and "Mind your own business!" at her mother.

Sara's mother tried nagging and ordering to get her daughter to treat her with more respect. "Stop that!" she would say. "You have no right to talk to me like that." At other times she would plead: "Please, Sara, I don't like it when you speak to me with so much hatred in your voice." These approaches were always ineffective. She next tried punishment.

"The next time you aren't nice to me," her mother threatened, "you're going to lose the privilege of watching television."

"You can't stop me from watching TV!" Sara angrily retorted.

Within an hour after this threat, an argument flared up between them. It culminated with Sara stomping off to her room and shouting "You're a bitch! I hate your f------ guts!"

Furious, her mother ran after Sara and pushed her down on the bed as she yelled, "That does it! I've warned you and now you've done it! You aren't watching TV in this house for a month! See if that doesn't teach you better respect!"

"Just shut up!" Sara screamed as her mother left the room crying and red-faced with anger.

It wasn't three days before Sara was watching TV whenever she pleased. Her mother was feeling desperate and helpless.

Obviously, there are many things wrong with the way Sara's mother approached the use of this discipline—among them her inability to calmly and rationally select a discipline, her inability to be specific about what she wanted to change, and her problem maintaining firmness and consistency.

The following example, also based on situations I have encountered while working with families, shows how this discipline technique can be used in a more controlled and effective manner.

Toby, at age fourteen, was beginning to go out more with friends. His parents were not sure he was mature enough to handle going out at night and tended to be restrictive about giving him greater freedom.

When Toby asked if he could go to a friend's house to spend the night, his parents were at first reluctant because they didn't know the friend, but they finally agreed he could go.

First, they clarified with him exactly what the two boys planned to do.

"We'll drop you off at Fred's house and then you're just going to be at his house playing video games and watching movies, right?" asked his mother.

"Yeah," replied Toby. "We're not going anywhere and Fred's mother will be home. There won't be any problems."

"Okay," said his father. "Then we'll pick you up tomorrow when you call us, and you've agreed to call by noon."

Later that evening, Toby's parents enjoyed the freedom of a night without Toby. They went to a movie and stopped at a convenience store for milk on their way home. As they drove up to the store, they noticed four boys sauntering out of the store. All were laughing, jostling each other, and smoking. One of the boys was Toby.

"I don't believe it!" his mother said as she and her husband watched the boys walk away from the store. As the car came to a stop in a parking place, Toby glanced over and recognized his parents' car. He was obviously astonished and, quickly regaining his composure, walked over and greeted them with, "Hi."

"Get in the car, Toby," his father said. "We'll take you home."

"Why?" asked Toby. "What's the problem?"

"You know very well what the problem is," said his mother, suddenly feeling both very angry and betrayed. The rest of the ride home was silent.

"Toby, we trusted you to go out and be where you said you would be," said his father when they were home. "Because you went someplace else, you're going to have to be punished. You will not be allowed to go out with your friends for two weeks."

"But, Dad," pleaded Toby, "it wasn't my fault. Honest. Fred and the other guys wanted to go to the store. What could

I do? I couldn't say I wouldn't go, could I? Besides, I was going to go to a movie with Paul next Tuesday."

"Our punishment still stands," said his mother evenly and calmly. "Perhaps this will help you learn that trust and honesty are very important to us." Toby understood that it was no use to argue further.

A year later, Toby, now fifteen, was able to go out with his friends one or two nights a week. His parents had no reason to believe that he ever violated the rule about doing exactly as he said he would when with his friends. One time he did decide to go to a video game arcade instead of to a movie. However, he called his parents from a public phone at the show, and they gave their permission and praised him for calling.

Sara's mother could have used this technique in an effective way by curtailing her nagging and giving orders only once, then following through. When Sara failed to follow an order or swore at her mother, a punishment (perhaps grounding or having the TV privilege taken away) should have been imposed, calmly and firmly, that would last a relatively short period of time. Her mother might have said, for instance, "You swore at me again and that means you stay in the house and off the phone for the night."

Every time Sara misbehaves, a consequence should follow. Her mother should stick to her word—if she says no phone use for two days, that's exactly what must happen. If Sara violates the terms of the punishment, then the punishment may be extended or increased: "I told you you were grounded to the house for two nights and I meant that. You left tonight and now you will not be going out this weekend."

5. Assign an Unpleasant Consequence

All punishments involve the deliberate infliction of pain or unpleasantness in order to change future behavior. Punishment always has an element of pain, loss, or suffering; therefore, it is unpleasant. There are other ways of inflicting unpleasantness in addition to time-out, removing rewards and privileges, and withholding friendliness. Each carries rules for effective use and risks when improperly used.

One is assigning an unpleasant consequence. This is a simple and well-known punishment. In fact, every school child is familiar with it; and certainly every motorist.

When teachers (and sometimes parents) assign the writing of sentences, they're using this technique. You hear children talk about this frequently: "You know how many sentences I had to write for Mr. Roberts? Five hundred! That sucks!"

Most readers are familiar with such time-honored (and often highly questionable) variations of this "noxious consequence" theme as making a child eat a cigarette, washing a child's mouth with soap, assigning extra chores (including scrubbing the bathroom floor with a toothbrush), making a child apologize to an enemy, or imposing a fine.

One of the serious risks with this punishment technique is that the unpleasant consequence can create additional problems. This is most likely to happen if the punishment is too severe. Then the child usually fails to complete the assignment, which leads to further punishment and ultimately rebellion against completing any punishment.

Moreover, normally intelligent and enterprising children, when assigned an unpleasant consequence, will try to figure out a shortcut to getting the task done quickly and with minimal pain or effort. That may involve an assembly-line approach to writing sentences (writing all the "I" words first, followed by all the "will" words, and so on) or an attempt to con someone else into doing it. Either way, instead of thinking about the offense and deciding never to do it again, the person being punished focuses the greatest amount of concentration on the question "How can I get this done without actually doing it?"

The other risk is that the child's relationship with the parent may be disturbed. This risk increases if the child regards the consequence as cruel, unusual, or harsh. Kids I've talked to who have been forced to eat cigarettes, smoke a pack of cigars, write thousands of sentences, or do arbitrary and overly tedious chores often harbor intense anger toward the adult who made them do it. Rarely are they angry at themselves for having done something wrong in the first place.

The motivation for assigning an unpleasant consequence is, of course, to discourage specific misbehavior. While I think this punishment can be effective with some children and teenagers, several conditions have to be met for it to work.

For this punishment to be effective, the child must have generally positive feelings and respect for the parent. As with all punishment, this one works better if it is given in the context of love, affection, and warmth.

The unpleasant consequence assigned must have a relationship to the offense and be perceived as fair by the young person. Being fined a quarter each time a child is caught swearing is likely to be seen as fair by many youngsters. Having their mouth washed with a strong soap is not. A child who has carelessly left the top off the trash can may not like picking up the trash that was scattered by a dog who got into the trash, but she would see it as a related punishment.

The assigned consequence should be of short duration. This is similar to the rule about severity. Moderate and short-term punishments will be more effective. If the consequence requires too many hours, days, or weeks to complete, the original reason for the unpleasant consequence may be lost on the child. Also, if this technique is used frequently, there is always a chance another misbehavior could occur and then one consequence follows on the heels of the last one. When punishments are too frequent or seem hopelessly long, children become discouraged.

6. Give More Than Enough

A less noxious and therefore less toxic way of inflicting punishment than assigning an unpleasant consequence I call giving more than enough.

The reasoning behind this discipline technique is fairly sound and based on research. When we are not allowed to do something, we yearn to do it. When we are given plenty of opportunity to do something, it becomes tiresome and less pleasurable.

This discipline technique can be illustrated by the following story. Michael is a ten-year-old who often disobeyed the rules at home. His parents made many rules for him, but Michael seemed to find ways of violating each and every one.

One day, after Michael had just gone outside to play, his father thought he smelled fire. He looked in Michael's room and discovered some recently burned matches on the floor. Investigating further, he found burned matches under the bed and on the floor of the closet. A few weeks before, Michael had been warned about playing with matches and told about the dangers of house fires.

After discussion with his wife, Michael's father decided to confront Michael about the match lighting—and to give Michael permission to light matches.

When Michael came in the house, his father was sitting at the kitchen counter, a new box of matches in front of him. The box held five hundred matches. He said to his son, "Michael, I found some burned matchsticks in your room. It's obvious you've been lighting matches even though both your mother and I warned you about fires and the danger to all of us.

"Now, if lighting fires and watching matches burn is so important to you," his father continued, "you can light all the matches you want. In fact, we want you to light some matches right now."

Michael sat sheepishly at the counter. He looked from his father to his mother and back to his father. "You mean you *want* me to light a match?"

"Yes," said his father, handing him a match, "you go ahead."

Michael scratched the match on the side of the box and it burst into a small flame. "Watch it burn and then blow it out," instructed his father. Michael complied.

"Now, light another one." Michael did it. "Now, another one," his father said. He asked Michael to light match after match, watch each burn, and blow it out.

After ten minutes, Michael asked, "How many more do I have to light? Can't I stop? This is getting stupid."

"It may seem stupid," his father said, "but we want you to keep lighting those matches until you are tired of it. And after this, if you want to light more matches, come back and let us know and we can sit around again and watch you light more matches. You can light as many as you like, just ask us first."

In all that night, Michael lit more than two hundred matches. As far as his parents knew, Michael never lit another match in the house without asking first. The problem was cured.

In this technique, the child is required to become satiated with a behavior so that it isn't thrilling, exciting, fascinating, disobedient, or sneaky fun anymore. Some parents have used this technique to stop screaming, whining, hitting ("Okay, you can hit. Hit this punching bag one hundred times"), smoking, and eating sweets.

As with other discipline and punishment techniques, this requires the cooperation of the child or adolescent. If the young person refuses to comply with the request or order ("You must smoke all of the cigarettes in this pack"), then a confrontation could evolve that brings about other kinds of punishment.

The young person must see the relationship between what she is asked to do and the behavior the parent wants to modify. If the child views the whole thing as illogical, cruel, or unfair, the technique will generate hostility toward the parent and may not stop the behavior but drive it underground.

WHEN CHILDREN CONTINUE to misbehave, despite the use of punishment, it is the parents' responsibility to ask the questions posed in chapter 3. In particular, the question of why she is acting like this needs serious consideration. Sometimes children misbehave because there are too many rules, too much control, and too little opportunity for self-expression or independence. Misbehavior cannot be seen only as a behavior to be stopped. The causes of that behavior must also be considered, especially if it is a recurring misbehavior.

Summary

You can discourage undesired and inappropriate behavior by using the following discipline techniques.

- Ignore the child.
- Withhold friendliness.
- Impose a time-out.
- Remove rewards and privileges.
- Assign an unpleasant consequence.
- Give more than enough.

T W E L V E

Techniques of Marginal Value

THERE ARE various discipline techniques that parents use regularly but that I cannot recommend without serious reservations. In contrast to the ten worst discipline techniques listed in chapter 2, these are not necessarily the most damaging parents can use. But they all pose considerable risks, which may overshadow the potential benefits they have.

Because they are so widespread and so many parents claim they are effective, they deserve to be discussed in a book on discipline. Yet all are double-edged swords—potentially effective, under very narrow circumstances; more likely harmful in most instances. I am including them here to illustrate ways they might be used with the least amount of damage to children.

1. Criticize Behavior

Useful criticism does not belittle or berate. Rather, it gives a child or adolescent an analysis of his behavior or conduct and lets him know where and how he has fallen short of the mark and of your expectations.

All parents criticize their children at times. It can be helpful to young people who have the self-esteem to learn from it without becoming defensive. It is a dangerous technique, though: When criticism is used too often or too harshly, it can damage a child's sense of self-worth. It must always be used in the context of a loving and caring parent-child relationship.

Here's an effective use of criticism:

After the Brumleys had visited relatives in another city, Mrs. Brumley felt she needed to say something to her sixteen-year-old daughter about her behavior during the visit. "Liza, I was so disappointed with the way you treated your cousin during our visit. You acted as if you thought Susan was a nerd and beneath you. We've tried to raise you so that you treat all people with respect and kindness. You were neither respectful nor kind to Susan."

Ideally, Liza's response to this kind of criticism should be something like: "I'm sorry, Mom, you're right. I shouldn't have been so mean to her. I felt bad about it even while I was doing it, but I couldn't stop myself."

In this ideal response, the young person expresses her realization that her parent is right and promises both her parent and herself that she will act differently in the future. Kids, of course, seldom respond in the ideal way. They can be defensive or angry if parents draw attention to a shortcoming.

Criticism usually works best with kids who are fairly secure, with adequate self-images and good self-esteem. They are the children or adolescents who need to be reminded of a failing or inadequacy so they can work harder to please their parents or live up to a family value.

Criticism will not be an effective discipline technique with an insecure youngster or one who is already too self-critical. Many children do not need to be harder on themselves; they need to be more accepting of their own shortcomings.

Angry and resistant kids are also not good candidates for criticism, it only makes them angrier. They often feel or believe they aren't loved, and criticism seems just another indication of that "fact." Likewise, children who blame others for their own problems will not respond well to criticism.

In general, the youngster who reacts well to criticism is the one who is reflective enough to look inward and to recognize that he needs to make some adjustments in his behavior.

There is a difference between criticism and belittling. When it is the child criticized and not the behavior, it is belittling. When a parent says, "How can you be so stupid?," it is belittling; "That wasn't the smartest thing you've done" is criticism. "You disgust me" is belittling; "The mess you left in the bathroom is disgusting" is criticism. Used properly, criticism tells something about the behavior. For instance, "Fighting is wrong. Problems can't be solved by getting into a fight."

It is easy to fall into the habit of criticizing our children's behavior too often. When criticism replaces the positive discipline techniques, then you run the risk of developing a hostile and more distant relationship with your child. To avoid this, use criticism infrequently, couch it in terms that show the young person you are not mad or upset with him as much as with his behavior and actions, and be sure to intersperse praise and other positive techniques.

No

2. Use Embarrassment

Many parents have told me that there's another discipline technique, somewhat like assigning responsibility, that works. It is embarrassing the child.

Some sincere and responsible parents report that they have used this technique with good results. The problem is that it must be timed perfectly and be used with the right child in the right situation so that it does not diminish a child's self-image or self-esteem. An added risk is that parents have to contrive an incident or scene to bring it about—and, as we all know, the best laid plans often go awry.

An example of the use of embarrassment in a fairly positive way occurred in the Miller family. Mrs. Miller had complained and offered various inducements in an effort to persuade her teenage daughter Sandy to clean her perpetually messy bedroom.

Although Sandy repeatedly promised to straighten up her room and seemed to have good intentions, the bedroom, if anything, appeared to get messier. Clothes were stacked on the floor; papers, books, and records were scattered everywhere. The closet was a shambles and the dresser top had not been seen in some time. Mrs. Miller had warned Sandy on more than one occasion that she would be embarrassed if one of her friends ever saw her cluttered, dirty room.

One day, Mrs. Miller had a bright idea. Instead of just threatening, why not let one of Sandy's friends actually see the room? A few days later, Alice, one of Sandy's classmates, called to arrange a Friday evening trip to the movies. Sandy wasn't home, but Mrs. Miller, quickly seizing the opportunity, invited Alice to come early on Friday evening and have dinner with the family before the girls left for the movie. Alice accepted.

On Friday night, Alice came for dinner and when she arrived, Mrs. Miller welcomed her and suggested she pop in on

Sandy, who was still in her room getting dressed.

When Sandy saw Alice, she was surprised and embarrassed by the disarray Alice witnessed. The girls left for the movie, but the next morning, after Sandy got up, she spent several hours rearranging and cleaning her bedroom. Mrs. Miller stayed out of her way and said nothing. But she smiled in triumph to herself—embarrassment had worked where nothing else she tried had brought about a change before.

To use embarrassment without causing serious damage to the self-esteem of a young person or to the relationship between a child and his parents requires that the issue chosen be one that will not lead to a personal crisis. It should also be one over which the young person has some control. The goal is not to make a young person so embarrassed that he withdraws from social contacts or contemplates suicide. Rather, it is to change a behavior without lasting emotional hurt.

Both adolescents and children will feel embarrassment and shame if some of their personal inadequacies are exposed to peers, favored relatives, or heroes. I believe that the risks are too great to use this technique with most young people and that there are enough other discipline techniques in this book that are more acceptable alternatives.

3. Make Threats

A threat is a statement by the parent informing the child of the consequences that will result from a particular action. As a warning, it might be useful. Indeed, many parents feel uncomfortable giving a punishment unless they have issued a warning first. As made by many parents, however, threats are a way of bullying children and using—or at least implying the use of—force and coercion. Therefore, parents who have a need to use power and authority may be inclined to use threats rather than some of the alternatives given in previous chapters.

Another problem develops when parents threaten but do not follow through. Suppose a boy has not kept his word when he says he will be at a friend's house and will call before he goes anywhere else. If his parents let him off with a threat ("We're warning you, if you ever do anything like this again, you're going to be grounded"), he may be willing to test this out and see what happens. And why not? He's already gotten away with it before. Maybe he can get away with it again.

A threat is effective only if the young person knows his parents fully intend to follow through. If they respond, after one threat, with a consequence, the child has no reason to test out their willingness to take action. He knows they will.

Threats that you have no intention of carrying out are worthless. Telling your daughter you will "kill" her if she has a bad report card is not likely to bring about the results you want. Scare tactics and impossible threats may have some short-term effect, but do not work in the long run.

If they are to be useful, threats should be specific. Don't just threaten that your child has to be "good or else." Instead, be specific about the behavior you want changed ("Be home by ten-thirty tonight . . .") and the consequences if your child doesn't heed the warning ("or you will have to go to bed early tomorrow night"). There is little room for misunderstanding the behavior you want to discourage when you are specific.

If parents use threats too often or rely on them too heavily, kids will usually react to them with resentment and even rebellion and defiance. Brad, a seventeen-year-old high school student, is an example of this. His father threatened that if Brad did not achieve all C's or better on his final report card of the year, he would not pay for Brad's car insurance, which would effectively ground Brad for the summer. Brad reacted with anger and a desire for revenge: "I'm not going to let him hold anything over my head," he said. "Maybe I'll fail two classes on purpose. Then he'll see he can't threaten me."

Threats have many drawbacks and few advantages. If used seldom, if the threatened consequence is reasonable, if the child knows you will follow through with your stated consequences, they could be effective. However, I believe there are many other alternatives that make the use of threats a marginal discipline technique.

4. Spank the Child

Some studies show that as many as 70 percent of parents have used physical punishment with kids. Many feel it is an effective and appropriate way to stop undesired behavior; others use it sparingly and feel guilty when they do. Either way, it's too potentially damaging to children to be recommended as a legitimate discipline technique.

As I have stated in previous chapters, the best methods of discipline are those that prevent problems, help children improve their self-control, and encourage desired behavior. If those discipline skills are used consistently, there is little reason to resort to punishments with most children, and little excuse to resort to spanking.

Even so, most parents do spank their kids at one time or another, and in recognition of this fact of life I'll suggest ways to use physical punishment to minimize its potential harm to kids.

First of all, it's important to distinguish spanking from other types of physical punishment. There are many forms of physical punishment. I hear from people—often from children—about parents who beat their children with belts, punch them with a closed fist, backhand them across the face, throw them against a wall, pull their hair, and twist their arms. One mother told me how she tried to wring her daughter's neck "like a chicken."

I can understand the overwhelming anger, frustration, desperation, and uncontrollable stress that leads to physical attacks on children and adolescents. Yet such attacks cannot be condoned or considered legitimate discipline techniques. They should be seen for what they really are: cruelty and a staggering inability on a parent's part to control temper and anger.

Physical attacks on children lead to hostility and anger and usually to a lowering of the youngster's self-esteem. In the long run, children who grow up on a steady diet of violent behavior either repeat this behavior with others or consider it their just due in life. Often they form relationships that involve violence and a punisher-victim dynamic.

In contrast, spanking as discussed here means a few well-controlled swats on the behind with an open hand. The child must be young, generally between three and five years of age. And this form of discipline should not be used more than a *very few* times in the child's life. One or two spankings early in childhood are not likely to leave most children with permanent emotional or physical scars. Beyond that very narrow definition, using any physical punishment is asking for trouble.

As with other punitive discipline techniques, physical punishment, even as narrowly defined here, carries many risks (not the least of which is parental guilt). For one thing, it almost always takes place when a parent is moved to extreme anger—and that's when things can easily get out of control. The same desperation and fury that lead you to spank as a "last resort" also increase the chances you'll spank too hard, use an instrument (like a belt) that will cause cuts or contusions, seriously hurt the child, or give the police or social service worker a reason to call on you and perhaps prosecute you for a criminal offense.

In addition, more often than not, spanking damages your relationship with your child. Children who receive physical punishment usually feel angry, hurt, and violated. They are likely to blame you for hurting them, rather than reflect on their misbehavior. They may think of ways of getting even with you or plan some form of revenge. Since children tend to withdraw from those who hurt them, they may hold their hostility inside and become more distant from you. As they get older, they may grow increasingly disobedient and cause you greater problems as a way of challenging your authority.

Like all forms of discipline, spanking, if used too often, loses its effectiveness. Certainly this is true as children get older. Not only does the hostility and resentment grow, but so does that child. The boy you could physically punish when he was in elementary school becomes the teenager who may be larger and more powerful than you. When parents continue to use physical punishment into adolescence, more force is required, and children turn on their parents. If you have relied on force and physical punishment, what do you have left when your fifteen-year-old son outweighs you by forty pounds and is four inches taller than you?

One of the things continued physical punishment teaches growing children is to solve problems with physical methods. Most parents would like to teach an opposite lesson. We want our children to learn to deal with problems without violence, fists, or guns. You cannot be a model of solving problems in nonviolent ways while using violence against your child.

All of this having been said, spanking has been known to be a quick way of getting a young child's attention and stopping misbehavior. But, like all the punishment techniques discussed in this book, physical punishment or spanking should be reserved only for dangerous, serious, or intolerable behavior. *Never use a discipline technique with such potentially serious consequences for a minor misbehavior.*

If you do opt to spank your child, try to follow these brief rules.

• Spank seldom and always use an open hand on the buttocks. Never spank or hit a child on any other part of the body. Never use an object other than the hand; using your hand ensures that you feel some pain and it is easier to judge how hard you are hitting. Use no more than three firm swats.

• Reserve spanking for very serious offenses, but only after you have tried many other discipline techniques. If you decide to spank, then do it immediately after a misbehavior.

• Finally, never spank or hit a child when you are too angry. If you find yourself resorting to hitting, spanking, or slapping when you are uncontrollably angry, you need professional help and should seek it immediately.

Summary

The discipline techniques in this chapter have questionable value and should be used only with extreme caution or not at all.

- Criticize behavior.
- Use embarrassment.
- Make threats.
- Spank the child.

THIRTEEN

How to Get Kids to Do What You Want Them to Do

IF THERE'S one universal question parents have, especially when they seek professional services, it's this: "How can I get my children to do what I say?" Usually when a mother or father brings a misbehaving child to a child-guidance clinic or psychologist, the complaint or problem is similar:

"He's got a mind of his own. He won't do anything I ask."

"She refused to obey the rules and she just wants to do what she wants to do!"

"He's defiant and won't do what we say. We give him everything, but he refuses to do anything we want him to do."

Children and teenagers may refuse to go to bed when they're supposed to, run away, come in later than curfew, steal, skip school, or hang around with the wrong friends. But all of these problems are variations on one basic theme: Children aren't doing what their parents want.

That's what this chapter is about. Also in a sense, that's what this whole book is about. How do you get your children to follow your rules, be generally compliant, and do things the way you want them done? In this chapter, I will present a checklist of ten steps you can follow to put together everything that has been discussed in the preceding chapters in order to get compliance from your children.

1. Establish Clear and Consistent Family Rules

Children need rules, and you as the parent must establish clear and consistent rules within the family. The rules should be spelled out explicitly so that children know exactly what you expect of them.

Do not change rules arbitrarily. Children have the right to know that your rules will be the same day after day. That makes them feel secure.

Sometimes parents lack the energy, time, or emotional resources to uphold and enforce rules consistently. Because of the high rate of divorce in this country, many parents live apart. Not only is there often conflict, hostility, and resentment between natural parents who are separated or divorced, but they may have different views of discipline.

Children need consistency in each house in which they live, as well as between parents who live apart. It's important for separated or divorced parents to bury the hatchet when it comes to raising the children and establish agreed-upon family rules for kids.

2. Select the Appropriate Discipline

One of the central themes of this book is that you must select the appropriate discipline technique to deal with the problem at hand and your particular child. To bring about and maintain desired and appropriate behaviors, you use one of the discipline techniques discussed in chapter 9. These are the positive discipline skills that encourage and reinforce "good" behavior. Such skills as giving praise, attention, encouragement, rewards, privileges, and suggestive praise will encourage or strengthen the behaviors you want. When you want to stop "bad" behavior, you use one of the discipline skills discussed in chapters 10 and 11. Such skills as ignoring, calling time-out, withdrawing rewards or privileges, and assigning unpleasant consequences are designed to correct and discourage inappropriate behaviors.

If you follow this format in dealing with your children, you have a way of deciding which discipline technique you should use to handle a behavior problem.

3. Stop Using the Ineffective and Often Destructive Discipline Techniques Described in Chapter 2

These are the so-called ten worst discipline techniques. You should stop using these because they do nothing to bring about compliance with your requests and may actually foster noncompliance. Yelling, nagging, hitting, and other counterproductive discipline skills have to go. Substitute the positive skills described in chapter 9.

4. Use Commands and Requests That Are Clear and Specific

Do not use vague or general commands and requests. Telling children to be "good" or to "change your attitude" leaves too much room for misunderstanding and differing interpretations—by both parent and child. It is preferable to be specific in giving directions to your children: "finish your school work," "hang up your clothes," and "come in the house to dinner" are more appropriate.

5. Use Appropriate Commands and Requests

Several things parents commonly do make it harder for their kids to comply with their requests and commands. One of these mistakes is to string together more than one request or command at the same time.

An example is: "Stop hitting your sister, leave the dog alone, and go to your room." Many children will not hear or remember more than one command and so are less likely to respond in the way you want. It is advisable to ask or order one thing at a time.

Another error is to ask a question when the child has no option—for instance, asking a child if she would like to do something—"Would you like to vacuum the carpet?" or "Would you mind cleaning the basement?" If this is a command rather than a request, then state it as such: "Pick up your toys, please."

Parents sometimes—perhaps out of an attempt to be polite or to soften the command—use "let's" commands: "Let's rake the leaves in the yard" or "Let's do the dishes." Again, this kind of command suggests that the child has an option. A common reaction is, therefore, "Let's not." Avoid the "let's" part of it and just say: "We're going out to rake the yard now."

One additional common error is giving reasons and rationales after making the command rather than before. For instance, a parent will say, "Change your clothes because we're having company tonight and we want you to look your best." If you are to include reasons for your commands, you should do so before rather than after your command. Say instead: "You and your sister are bothering each other. Move over to the dining room table and take your baseball cards with you."

6. Make Requests Only Once

Many parents start to lose control by repeatedly asking a child to comply with a request ("I've asked you several times to get ready for bed. Don't make me tell you any more!"). If you've made a command or a request several times, your child probably knows you're going to continue to make the same request. Why should she respond this time or the next? She knows she's got plenty of chances.

That's where this rule about compliance is so important. Ask once. If you make a second request, you might as well be prepared to ask a third, fourth, or fifth time. From there it's only a short step to the ineffectual cycle of endless nagging. To avoid that, make one request and then take action. This calls for you to be firm and consistent. You must not be afraid to take action to bring about compliance with your usual requests.

7. Allow a Reasonable Amount of Time for Children to Comply

We don't necessarily want to produce children who are automatons that jump when we say jump. On the other hand, we do want children who respond to our reasonable requests, commands, and rules. While it's usually too much to ask children to respond within seconds, you do expect a response in a relatively short period of time.

If a child is watching a particularly interesting TV program or about to rack up her highest score ever on her favorite video game, it might be the wrong time to remind her that she forgot to feed the dog. Besides that, it usually doesn't matter when the garbage is taken out or the bed is made. So, wait until there's a commercial on TV or the video game has ended. Then it is fair to expect that the young person will do what you ask before beginning another activity. Be sure that you are not making an unreasonable demand or always expecting instant compliance.

8. Use Positive Discipline Techniques When Children Do What You Ask

When you make a request and your child responds well, use one of the positive skills—praise, attention, encouragement, rewards, privileges, or suggestive praise—to let your child know you recognize her compliance and approve of it. Not only do you approve, but you want her to continue to do what you ask. "Hey, you got your pajamas on when I asked you to. That's great! How about if I read to you tonight for a while?" Chances are the next time you tell her to get ready for bed, she will be more likely to respond in the way you desire.

9. Use Negative and Punishing Techniques When Children Do Not Respond in the Way You Have Asked

When your child does not do what you have asked, then you must take action. You must use a negative or punishing technique to let her know that noncompliance gets punished.

Instead of giving praise and attention, impose time-out or remove a reward or privilege to deal with noncompliance. "Since you did not get your pajamas on when I asked you to, you will have to go to bed earlier tomorrow night." Or, "Since you did not get your pajamas on when I asked, I cannot read you a story tonight."

10. Don't Make Too Many Requests

Don't ask children to do things too often. This is advisable particularly if they have a problem with compliance. Children who are asked too often or have too many demands placed upon them often rebel.

If you are trying to teach your child to be more compliant, then start with perhaps two or three requests a day. Use plenty of positive techniques when she responds. As she does better, you can safely increase the number of requests you make each day. But don't forget to continue using the reinforcing and positive skills as she continues to do what you ask.

LEARNING HOW to put all the discipline skills together to bring about compliance with rules, commands, and requests will make you a better parent and help you to see your children as more delightful, more respectful, and easier-to-manage kids.

Summary

To get kids to do what you want them to do more often, follow these ten steps.

1. Establish clear and consistent family rules.
2. Select the appropriate discipline techniques.
3. Stop using ineffective and often destructive discipline techniques.
4. Use commands and requests that are clear and specific.
5. Use appropriate commands and requests.
6. Make requests only once.
7. Allow a reasonable amount of time for children to comply.
8. Use positive discipline techniques when children do what you ask.
9. Use punishment techniques when children do not comply.
10. Don't make too many requests.

FOURTEEN

What to Do If Nothing You Try Works

I'VE HEARD many parents say "Nothing we try seems to work" or "I'm at the end of my rope! I can't do anything with that kid!" Occasionally parents throw up their hands in complete frustration and resignation and say: "I've had it! The next time he tells me I can't make him stay home and he leaves the house, I'm calling the police. Let them deal with him; I can't anymore!"

Frequently when parents say they've tried everything, they haven't. That's one of the reasons I wrote this book. I wanted to let parents know the various kinds of discipline they could be using but often aren't. I wanted them to have hope, to discover alternative forms of discipline, and most of all to have somewhere to turn when they felt as if they were losing control of a child.

Sometimes parents have indeed tried many forms of discipline and still can't reach a child or get him to conform to reasonable requests, demands, limits, or rules. That's what this chapter deals with: What do you do when you've tried everything and nothing is working? Here are some rules of thumb to follow when you've reached the end of your patience and you just don't know where else to turn.

Have You Really Tried Everything?

If you feel totally frustrated and have exhausted the discipline alternatives, go back through this book. Reread chapters 6 through 11 and make sure you have followed the discipline guidelines and used the types of discipline described. Have you tried not just punishment, but the positive parenting skills? Have you tried not just two, three, or four discipline techniques, but ten or fifteen?

Are You Using the Discipline Skills in the Right Ways?

Each discipline technique has a set of guidelines that go with it. Are you following those guidelines so the discipline you use really does have a chance to be successful? Or are you sabotaging or undermining your own efforts by ignoring the guidelines? If you find that you haven't been using certain discipline skills in the right ways, try again and give the discipline and your child another chance.

Is Your Child Really Beyond Your Control?

Parents frequently complain they have lost control of a child, but when they examine the situation objectively they can see that the young person is still basically compliant even if aspects of his behavior need improvement.

Your teenage son may not respond to your requests to clean his room or turn down the stereo, but he still goes to school, holds down a job, and comes in at curfew. Your daughter may have considerable conflict with one parent, refusing to obey or being disrespectful, but have good relationships with school teachers and friends. Some young people whose parents describe them as incorrigible seem to me to be pretty good kids, willing to obey rules and follow requests when there is some indication they are loved, appreciated, or treated with respect.

I can point to dozens of examples from my experiences with troubled families to show that kids whose parents have essentially given up on them can make outstanding reversals in their behavior. One such case is Andrew, a sixteen-year-old whose parents said he was incorrigible. They came to see me when they were contemplating filing a complaint against him in juvenile court.

Andrew was indeed acting in a way that seemed destined to get him into a juvenile detention center. He was skipping school, acting disrespectful to his teachers, drinking (and driving), shoplifting, staying out past his parents' curfew, and continually alienating his parents through his blatant disregard for their rules or their feelings. His parents were angry and upset most of the time. They felt they could not communicate with Andrew and believed the next step was to put him in the hands of the juvenile court.

I decided I wouldn't work with Andrew at all. I would, instead, meet regularly with his parents to help them make changes in their ways of handling Andrew.

In my sessions with his parents, we discussed discipline techniques, communication patterns, and their expectations for Andrew. They examined their rules and how they communicated these rules to their son. They also changed some of their typical discipline techniques. They stopped criticizing and nagging Andrew. They also stopped using lectures, threats, and physical punishment. Their discipline became more consistent, and communication improved dramatically.

Within a year, Andrew's behavior looked a lot different to his parents. Andrew and his parents were talking to each other. Andrew accepted rules; when he wanted to stay out past his curfew, for instance, he called to ask if it would be all right for him to come in later than agreed. He was attending school regularly, holding down his first job, and being very responsible about work. Andrew did not appear to be an incorrigible son at all. His parents were very pleased with how *he* had changed.

Young people who seem to have severe behavior problems often are reacting to inconsistent and inappropriate discipline and handling by their parents. If you have really considered this and it seems a possible explanation for your child's problems, then it may be time to seek the services of a professional who can help change your discipline techniques. That could mean seeing a family counselor, a child psychologist, or a psychotherapist experienced in dealing with parents, families, or children.

Many parents feel a sense of shame if they have to admit their child has a problem they cannot handle. We all like to think we are exceptional (or at least adequate) parents and our children won't have the problems other children have. But this is not always true. Even the best of parents sometimes find they have a youngster who is too difficult to handle without guidance. In order to make use of professional help, you will have to swallow your pride and admit that sometimes we all need help. (Even psychologists and psychotherapists frequently have to see other professionals for family problems.) It's not a matter of shame. More, it is a wise set of parents who agree they have done what they know how to do and now they need to rely on someone else to help them understand what they can best do.

Another thing many parents feel is that raising children should somehow come naturally or that family problems should be kept in the family. "I don't want someone outside of this family telling me how to raise my kids" is a common attitude. As a result, a sense of denial may set in so that the problems continue and no help is sought. Raising children is not an easy matter, and most of us, even if we feel it should come naturally, frequently need to turn to someone who deals with the problems of parenting every day to assist us in coming up with some answers or a new direction. Most competent psychologists and psychotherapists aren't going to tell you how to raise your kids. They may point out some things that are interfering with harmony in the family, or they may suggest some new options on how to handle discipline.

Before making the decision to request professional help, you might ask yourself the following questions in an effort to be as objective as possible about your youngster's problems.

How Old Was My Child When the Problems Started?

Some problems have to do with the child's age or development level. It is normal for two- or three-year-olds to go through a negative stage as they learn to master their environment; the word "No!" is a favorite staple in their vocabulary. That doesn't mean there is anything wrong with your child or you as a parent. At about age ten, many children become more sensitive and prone to emotional upset. They may cry more and have more trouble handling stress. At age eleven, many children are more hyperactive, have problems in their relationships with peers (especially of the opposite sex), and don't settle down to their school work with any great consistency. Middle teenagers begin to break away from their parents and seek greater independence. They are more interested in friendships and peer relationships than in family togetherness. They may rebel against the rules and request more freedom.

All this is normal and expected behavior and does not indicate a conduct or behavior problem.

How Long Has the Problem Gone On?

The longer a problem has persisted, the more likely it represents something serious rather than just a passing phase, a developmental stage, or a temporary maladjustment. Problems at the beginning of the school year may be expected to end in a few days or at most a week or so. Following the loss of a friend or relative, a child may be expected to be depressed or moody for a few days or weeks. If these kinds of problems go on too long, a more serious issue may be involved.

What Type of Problem Is It?

The type of problem should be considered. Certain problems are usually minor, even if they do persist over a longer period of time. Nail biting, thumb sucking, and bed-wetting, even when they go on for a long period, may not be indications of a need for professional assistance. Running away, suicidal threats, stealing, refusal to eat, and aggression may be indications of serious problems even when they have gone on for only a very short period of time.

What Are the Known Reasons for Problems?

If a reason for a problem is known, it may be less serious than if it seems to develop for no known reason. A child may come back regularly from a visit with a noncustodial parent feeling moody, irritable, and out-of-sorts. But if a child becomes more difficult to live with for no known reason, it should be of greater concern to a parent.

What Has Happened When You've Tried to Solve the Problem Before?

The first thing most parents do when a problem occurs is to see if it goes away on its own. If it doesn't then discipline or correction is in order. Parents may turn to a spouse, friends, relatives, or others for guidance. If the problem persists, they may attempt to get advice from a minister, priest, or psychotherapist. This is a reasonable chain of events. But if all attempts prove unsuccessful, then the problem should certainly be considered much more serious.

Where do you turn for help? There are many therapeutic approaches available. With the ready access to mental health clinics, psychologists, psychiatrists, social workers, mental health counselors, school counselors, and ministers or priests trained in counseling and guidance, it is generally easy to locate a trained professional through referral from a friend, doctor, or minister.

That doesn't mean that the therapist to whom you are first referred will be best for you or your child. Not every therapist or psychologist works with families or children. Some know very little about discipline or how to deal with children's behavior problems. Also, whether a therapist is a psychiatrist, psychologist, social worker, or mental health counselor may not matter nearly as much as such issues as quality of work, area of expertise, experience with children, and effectiveness with the kind of problem your child has.

Accepting that your child has a serious problem and that your legitimate efforts at changing your discipline to meet the problem have failed is the first step. Coming to terms with this and asking for professional help is the next step. However, allowing a problem to go on too long may make it more difficult for you and your child to overcome.

Sometimes a child's behavior or conduct problems are

beyond the help a parent can offer or the scope of the ability of a psychotherapist—even with regular, intense, or frequent therapy sessions. Children and teenagers who are beyond their parents' control may need the services of a child treatment center, a residential facility, or the local juvenile or family court. The decision to take these more drastic and extreme measures should probably be made with a psychotherapist. But by going to a professional early enough you may be able to make the changes needed within the family so that these more drastic steps are entirely unnecessary.

SUGGESTED READING

General Parenting Books

Brazelton, T. Berry. *Toddlers and Parents*. New York: Doubleday, 1989.

Dinkmeyer, Don, Sr., and Gary D. McKay. *Systematic Training for Effective Parenting Parent's Handbook*. Circle Pines, Minn.: American Guidance Services, 1989.

Dodson, Fitzhugh. *How to Parent*. New York: New American Library/Signet, 1971.

————. *How to Father*. New York: New American Library/Signet, 1975.

Faber, Adele, and Elaine Mazlish. *Liberated Parents—Liberated Children*. New York: Avon Books, 1976.

Green, Christopher. *Toddler Taming*. New York: Fawcett, 1985.

Ilg, Frances L., and Louise Bates Ames. *Child Behavior*. New York: Harper and Row, 1982.

Books About Childhood Development

Brazelton, T. Berry. *Infants and Mothers: Differences in Development*. New York: Delta Books, 1983.

Spock, Benjamin. *Baby and Child Care*. New York: Simon and Schuster/Pocket Books, 1981.

Steinberg, Laurence, and Ann Levine. *You and Your Adolescent: A Parent's Guide for Ages Ten to Twenty.* New York: Harper and Row, 1990.

While, Burton L. *The First Three Years of Life.* Englewood Cliffs, N.J.: Prentice-Hall, 1987.

Discipline and Child-Rearing Books

Canter, Lee, and Marlene Canter. *Assertive Discipline for Parents.* Santa Monica, Calif.: Canter and Associates, 1982.

Clark, Lynn. *The Time-Out Solution: A Parent's Guide for Handling Everyday Behavior Problems.* Chicago: Contemporary Books, 1989.

Dobson, James. *Dare to Discipline.* Wheaton, Ill.: Tyndale, 1973.

Dreikurs, Rudolf, and Vicki Stolz. *Children: The Challenge.* New York: Dutton, 1987.

Garber, Stephen, Marianne D. Garber, and Robyn F. Spizman. *Good Behavior: Over 1200 Sensible Solutions to Your Child's Problems from Birth to Age Twelve.* New York: Villard Books, 1987.

Lickona, Thomas. *Raising Good Children.* New York: Bantam Books, 1985.

Rosemond, John. *Six-Point Plan for Raising Happy, Healthy Children.* Kansas City: Andrews and McMeel, 1989.

Williamson, Peter. *Good Kids, Bad Behavior.* New York: Simon and Schuster, 1990.

Books for Improving Communication

Ginott, Haim G. *Between Parent and Child.* New York: Avon, 1976.

Gordan, Thomas. *Parent Effectiveness Training: The Tested New Way to Raise Responsible Children.* New York: McKay, 1970.

Behavioral Techniques in Parenting Books

Becker, Wesley C. *Parents Are Teachers: A Child Management Program.* Champaign, Ill.: Research Press, 1971.

Patterson, Gerald R. *Living with Children.* Revised ed. Champaign, Ill.: Research Press, 1976.